SECURE

SURVIVE

THRIVE

HOW TO GET INTO

RECRUITMENT,

SURVIVE YOUR PROBATION AND SMASH YOUR TARGETS IN YOUR FIRST 12 MONTHS!

STEPHEN JOSEPH

SECURE SURVIVE THRIVE
HOW TO GET INTO RECRUITMENT, SURVIVE YOUR
PROBATION AND SMASH YOUR TARGETS IN YOUR FIRST 12
MONTHS!

Author: STEPHEN JOSEPH

© Stephen Joseph

First published - 2019

CROWDSOURCED CORRECTIONS

Attention all word warriors and grammar junkies

Thank you for purchasing my book. I really hope you enjoy it and, more importantly, that it helps you be more successful in recruitment. Whist this book was never intended to be a literary masterpiece, I have made every effort to ensure it is as correct as possible.

The book has been through a number of rounds of editing and proofreading before publishing; however, it's still possible you might spot the odd typo. If you do, I welcome you to get in touch via my LinkedIn page (https://www.linkedin.com/in/stephen-joseph-a5637442) so we can amend it on the next version.

CONTENTS

CONTENTS

SECURE SURVIVE THRIVE

HOW TO GET INTO RECRUITMENT, SURVIVE YOUR PROBATION AND SMASH YOUR TARGETS IN YOUR FIRST 12 MONTHS!

STEPHEN JOSEPH

Chapter **1**

Introduction

Welcome to Secure, Survive, Thrive: How to Get into Recruitment, Survive your Probation Period and Smash your Targets in Your First 12 Months! My name is Stephen Joseph and I'm the author of this book.

This book should be viewed as a practical reference text to help you *secure* your first recruitment role.

I'll tell you about myself in a moment; however, it was certainly difficult for me to get my first role. I had to overcome a lot of challenges to get into recruitment. So, I share the methods I used to do that.

Equally, if you are currently in a recruitment role, or you've recently started and you're in your first two or three months, or anything under six months (i.e. inside the probation window), and you're concerned you're not on the right track, there will be a lot of advice for you to take control and get things heading in the right direction.

That's kind of my specialty, working with those people who have started to go down the wrong path and need help. That is part of the *survive* section of the book, I guess. The survival of your first 3-6 months!

Ultimately, we're hopefully looking for a bit more than survival (although that would be achievement enough in recruitment). I guess to ***thrive*** is really what we're looking for. And with that, really, I want you to finish this book, apply the advice and techniques you will learn, set yourself some objectives to work towards, and start to move closer towards becoming a top producer.

If you have the right head on your shoulders, and you once believed you could do it but your confidence has been knocked within your first two or three months and that initial drive to become a top producer has faded, then I'm here to tell you it's not an elitist group. It's actually mostly just hard work, dedication and clear focus.

I'm going to tell you the tips, tricks, and the industry hacks that I learned over the years to help you **thrive** in your first twelve months. I'm going to teach you how to become a top producer. And, by the way, you can become a top producer in a much shorter time than your managers or the current top biller would have you believe.

So, there it is. We're going to cover practical advice on how to secure your first role, some solid advice on how to survive your probation and finally how to go on and thrive in your first year, taking down every record on the way.

Who is this book for?

As the title would suggest this book was designed for people who are undertaking their first recruitment role or those who are in or around their first twelve months. You will usually be one of the three following types of people:

1. First Jobbers

This book is for anyone who is looking to secure their first job in the recruitment sector. You may be in your first real job after graduating, or you may have some work experience in customer service, sales, retail etc., but this is your first serious job. If you're in this category you're likely to be under 25.

2. Second Jobbers

This book is also for anyone who is a second jobber. Maybe you've had a previous career and you're looking to convert to recruitment. This could be all manner of people, including those who graduated, took a career in their studied field, but didn't enjoy it (usually family pressures) and want to try something else, or anyone who has reached a financial or skill ceiling in their current role and has enough time, energy or money to try something new. This was me, as I'll explain.

3. Last Chancers

If you have had two or three short stints in recruitment and it hasn't worked out, you would be what I could call a last chancer. Either you have been made redundant or let go. You are often the type that will be in denial about what actually happened. You will also be prime rec2rec (recruitment to recruitment is a sector that specialises in placing recruitment consultants at recruitment agencies) bait now!

The last scenario is quite common. If this describes you or your situation then you may have dodged a bullet in picking up this book and you *might* still have a chance!

What often happens is that people spend between three to six months in any given role and don't progress as quickly as their employer wants or they lack the sales they need to survive and they have to move on for one reason or another. Often this is as much your employer's fault as yours. However, it is you that will be left without a job.

So, if the last one is you, then you are likely to get the most value out of this book. If you're one of the first two, then your objective is not to be number three!

Who is this book not for?

If you are a top producer, or you're already a sales manager, you're still likely to get a lot of benefit from this book (especially in the Thrive section), but it's not hugely targeted at you; it is Secure, Survive, Thrive. So, its core message will have the most value to those people inside their first 12 months, although I welcome anyone to read it and pass it amongst your friends and colleagues.

Let's move on and let me introduce myself.

Chapter **2**

About Me

I guess it's fitting for any author of a self-help or expert book to tell you a little about themselves to give you the faith to warrant reading on.

The easiest way to do that is to start by saying that this book is exactly the kind of book that would have helped me a decade ago. There is a lot that people don't tell you about the recruitment game that might put some of you off getting involved in the first place, and some that will make you question your desire to stay in this industry.

Recruitment was a second career for me. It wasn't my first forte. I am a self-confessed second jobber. I didn't go to recruitment after leaving university or school. I went into motor trade parts sales to begin with. I did this successfully for about ten years, so I certainly had sales work experience behind me. I had a fantastic work ethic and I was a top performer. I had awards and achievements to list. It should have been a straightforward transition over to recruitment. At least, that's what I thought

I was attracted, probably like you, to the bright lights of the city, the lustre, the culture, and, most importantly, the money that recruiting supposedly brings.

After all, you just send off a few CVs, wait for a little while, and then you get paid, right? And most advertised "trainee recruitment" roles still today promise in excess of hundreds of thousands of pounds in a relatively short period of time.

So, if you are young, wet behind the ears, and money-driven like I was, I'm sure you were picking up the lie just as quickly. However, you're probably finding, much like I did, that securing your first recruitment job, especially if you're not a 2:1 graduate from a Russell Group university with sales experience behind you, is not that easy. Recruitment hiring managers are exactly like the hiring managers you will speak to, and they are not straightforward people. They like an easy ride just as much as anyone else and they want an easy lay down on the CV. What that means is they're looking for someone that's as easy as possible to convert into cash, and most of us, especially at the trainee level, are not that. So, you need to display yourself in the right way.

When I started applying for trainee roles, I applied for tens, maybe hundreds of jobs. All trainee recruitment roles, all promising training with no experience needed, and yet none of them would hire me. I didn't have the experience that they wanted, and so I found out quickly it wasn't going to be that easy.

In the end, after changing my CV using the techniques that I demonstrate later in this book, I managed to secure my first interview and secured my first job, again using the techniques I'm about to share with you. Even then, I found it was such a ferocious industry. They were hiring six people. I later found out they only planned to keep the best two. Four of the six were given full-time, permanent jobs, and two of us were given 1-month internships. Yep, you guessed it. That was me. I wasn't even good enough for a job! I guess I know now that I was a "punt".

Anyway, after the internship both myself and James (the other candidate) secured permanent jobs. I'd love to tell you that was the end of the struggle and I went on to be top biller. However, that wasn't the case. Once I got into that job it was still very difficult for me. In fact, the first six months were nothing short of a hell. Hence, the second part of my title. Survive, because that's what we'll be looking to do first of all.

Well, what happens to a guy they take a punt on, who isn't doing very well? I got put on performance management and I almost got dismissed from my first role. So, if anyone is a good testament to write a book on how to survive, it's definitely me.

From that turning point I managed to turn the job around. I went on to become *a* top producer, then *the* top producer, then team leader and divisional manager in a very short period of time. I think recruitment has a way of testing how much you want it before it gives you anything. This was all at a small boutique recruitment company. After getting to the top of the tree and starting to rest on my laurels a little, I knew I had to move on to a bigger pond.

I decided to take the biggest leap of my career again and leave all the success behind to go and start a brand-new business for a bigger firm that didn't have a presence in London. I pretty much started a business from scratch with financial backing from a bigger recruitment firm in the most competitive recruitment place in the world; London. Fast forward 5 years and that business is now more than twelve consultants strong and delivers well in excess of a million pounds in gross profit (GP) a year. I took the business from an office not much bigger than your sister's box room to a beautiful space overlooking the city of London.

That's a little bit about my journey and why I'm just the one to advise you. Along the way, I managed to pick up a whole host of accolades, I've won several awards for being a top-producing consultant, top-producing branch, best manager etc. I've managed to join various sales achievers' clubs, I have eaten at countless Michelin starred restaurants, and I was invited to be one of the four members to be given equity in the business, which we sold a short while back for just under £40m in a management buyout with Yorkshire Bank and Investment group Tosca.

So, I know everything about the business, from training new recruiters and developing them into top industry performers, how to hire, train, and motivate staff, and how to add value to your company to increase its multiple at exit, making it attractive to banks and private equity houses. Furthermore, I would like to say I did all that in my own ethical way. I didn't cross any borders, I respected my restrictive covenants, I've built a successful temp desk more than three times, and, perhaps more importantly than all of that, I still hold accounts today that I held eight or nine years ago. So, if you're about talking the talk and walking the walk, hopefully that will give you the confidence you need to believe I can help you on your path.

Let's move on now to find out what you can really expect in recruitment and we will find out if you still want to do it!

Chapter

The truth about recruitment and what you can really expect

Welcome to the ugly world of recruitment, and I say that because it is an ugly world. Depending on the company you get into, the culture, the environment, their training (or lack of), all determines if you're going to have a good time or a horrible time. However, there are some things that are definitely going to be true, so I'll cover the basics.

Now let's see if I can put you off.

What can you expect? Definite pros and cons and highs and lows. The highs are really high and the lows are really low. Every day and week will take you from feeling on top of the world to nearly walking out.

Let me give you an indication of what life's likely to be like and then you can make your own decision about whether you see fit to continue in this industry.

Hours

First of all, in terms of hours you can forget what the contract says, no matter how flexible they claim it can be, or if they say they allow some people to leave at certain times and still get their work done. For you as trainee recruiters, you're going to need to do more than what the contracted hours say. You're going to need to be sinking anything from eight to twelve hours per day in your first six months as a general rule.

If you're not, then I would question how much you're really getting done. When you start you are likely to be slow and inefficient. The simplest way to combat this is to use more time. As your skill increases and you think you can start to leave 'on time', your pipeline will increase duly, and naturally you will have more to do, so leaving early will be null and void again. So, in short, you can forget what the contracted hours say. They're not going to be relevant. They're primarily applicable for payouts in cases of dismissal, sickness, redundancy etc. Regardless of what they say, forget it. You're going to need to do at least eight to twelve hours per day.

Pressure

I'm sure you would have heard that it's not an easy job and you have no idea how difficult it's going to be until you get in there. However, I can tell you it is going to be far more difficult than you can imagine. Essentially, the pressure is going to be on you at all times to deliver. If you're in one of the smaller firms, or perhaps one that arguably has a better culture, then that's almost going to be worse. They're going to give you almost no pressure at all, but it's going to be building in the background and you're not going to know it. One day, somebody is going to bring you into an office to have a "conversation" and you're going to have a week to turn things around before you're out the door. Even if you're not feeling it, believe me, it's there.

The simple fact is we are in a business where delivery is what pays us. We are not stacking shelves in supermarkets, we're not putting things away, we're not farming, and we're not laying floors. There is no value in your work unless you deliver. Once again, I don't care if you're the best at filing or tidying or you always get the milk or pick up the fruit allocation for the office. There's no lasting value in any of those tasks. We are salespeople in this business and your value is when you convert a candidate into cash in the form of a temp placement or a permanent fee.

I'm sorry to say it, but other than your placements, as billing headcount you are just cost. If you are in the resourcing side it may be slightly different, but if you're a consultant you are hired to make placements and you are expected to deliver.

So, what's the antidote for the ever-building pressure?... Delivery. The more you can deliver, the quicker you can deliver it, and the greater quantities that you can deliver, the less pressure will be on you and the more will be applied to someone else. So, the pressure is going to be there, and it's going to remain consistent for at least your first six to twelve months, maybe eighteen if you take a slower path.

Mentally Draining

We have covered the hours, however, if you're new to recruitment and you have worked in a bar, for example, you might be thinking, "Well, I have done twelve hour shifts and I have been on my feet for hours and I survived okay, so I should be fine, right?" Let me address that. The hours here are not those kind of hours. It's not like working a long day labouring onsite. You don't go home feeling physically drained but believe me you will go home mentally drained. Absolutely no question about it. You think your Fridays are going to be partying and, believe me, there will be some of that. But in the early days, at least if you're pushing enough to become a top biller, you're more likely going home and falling asleep by nine-o-clock on the sofa on a Friday because you're mentally frazzled.

11

Building a desk is a long, laborious task and it takes a lot of mental pressure, which, combined with the hours and rejection over a sustained period, takes its toll. I've seen women <u>and</u> grown men break down and cry. I have seen people turn to drink or drugs as a coping mechanism, all within their first twelve months, because the game has gotten them down so much that they've got no physical energy left, no mental energy left, and they're at rock bottom. Then something else happens and it just breaks them down. If you think you're stronger than that, good. I'm pleased to hear it. However, believe me, you need to be prepared because it's not going to be an enjoyable experience in your first six months.

Misconceptions you may have about recruiting

I know sales. I'll get it quickly.

If you're an accomplished salesperson, you might be thinking, "Well, you know, I'm aware of sales pressure. I'm pretty confident in my ability. I should be okay." Recruitment sales is an unusual beast. It's not like anything you've ever done or come across before.

We're selling a service here. We're not selling a product. It's very difficult for you to say that your product is bigger, badder, faster, or cheaper than your rivals because, truthfully, it's unlikely to be and, even if your company claims it has an advantage over a rival, it's likely to be insignificant. Your client isn't going to care anywhere near as much as you will. You are not going to have those kinds of distinct advantages. You're selling them something that might happen in the future, i.e. "When you next have a need, could you call us?" and then you need to maintain that relationship. It's a very unusual way of selling, but the key thing to remember in this part is we're selling a relationship here, not a physical product.

For example, if you are on what I call a 'one bang sale' where you have a customer in front of you, you give them your best 'spiel', then they buy it, or they don't. Once they've bought it, you ring it up. If they don't, they leave and you go to your next one. That's what many of you would have done in call centre environments and in door-knocking. They are one bang sales. That's the ultimate standard sale, and in that, there's basically a formula. If you do x number of calls, you're likely to make y number of sales, and to increase that, you need to increase your skill or you need to increase your dial rate. It's straightforward. It's an expected number.

In recruitment, we're not talking about a one bang sale. We're talking about a relationship, and it's very difficult to control that relationship. Say you manage to get a vacancy from a client and you manage to sufficiently shortlist the role. You have some good candidates and they go to an interview. You've got a deal that looks like a lay-down. You've got a fantastic candidate to fill into the role, he's well prepped, he turns up on time. Everything is going in your favour. For you, this is a massive deal. Your first deal over the line! Now all we need to do is wait for the confirmation that he got the job. Then you learn he walked into the interview and dropped a c-bomb, he turned up smelling of booze, or he wasn't wearing a tie and the hiring manager thinks that's a must. That's it. It's game over. No deal. He's not that bothered. He will get another role. However, you're bothered; you just lost your deal. And if that happened to be the deal you needed to hit the target or that would keep you in the job, it's an even bigger deal!

That is another reason why the job is mentally draining; the ultimate outcome, the final hurdle that stands between you securing your sale or not is totally out of your control! Now, of course there are ways to overcome and minimise (which we will cover later in the book) but once again you can see how this is going to take its toll on you.

But you get to help people and have that warm fuzzy feeling, right?

Another common misconception is that you get a warm and fuzzy feeling when your candidate says yes, punches the air and secures their dream job. If you're coming into recruitment with a view that you'd love to help people secure and find the perfect job, I'm very happy for you and I'd love that to be the case and, believe me, in some cases that does happen. But if you're under the impression that you're going to get people into their perfect job and they'll be forever grateful to you and they'll be showering you with gifts and gratitude… that just doesn't happen. Well, not very often anyway. In a fast-paced temp recruitment firm you will get a couple of them a year.

Now this point can vary from sector to sector, however, in the vast majority of mainstream temp sectors it's true. What's more likely in most sectors is you're helping a temp get back into a role. More often than not, they'll resent you for it because you will need to control pay and charge and that might not be exactly what they wanted. Instead of gratitude, there are usually obstacles to overcome to even get them to accept it.

So, if you're coming into recruitment to tick the box of helping people, though this does happen, it definitely shouldn't be your driving force because it just doesn't happen anywhere near as often as you think.

I want to use recruitment as a leapfrog into HR.

Lastly, if you're getting into recruitment because you'd like to look at a career in HR and you think that recruitment is part of a HR function, that's the wrong train of thought. HR and recruitment are linked. Recruitment is part of the HR function, and recruiters definitely have some HR stuff that we need to work around, but fundamentally we want opposite things. For the most part, HR people would rather not deal with recruiters, and, frankly, we would rather not deal with HR people if we could avoid it.

If you are thinking that you can use recruitment as a link to HR, well, again, it's been done and it's possible, but it's not the right path. If you want to succeed, that's a different train of thinking. Recruitment is first and foremost a sales role. If you get asked that question in an interview, which they sometimes do, remember this.

Recruitment is sales.

It's nothing else. It's not a HR job. If you come into it from anything but that point of view, you're on the wrong path.

So, to wrap up, we've discussed the negatives. Recruitment is a wonderful job if you can get your head around it. When you can get on a winning streak, there is no greater job. The highs are so high, the lows are unbearably low, but when you think about the earning potential for such a low barrier to entry job, it really is beautiful. If the aforementioned statements haven't put you off, then you're on the right pathway. So, let me help you secure your first role and let me tell you how to get ready for your interviews.

SECURE

Time : Pre-employment

Objective: To increase your odds of securing your first recruitment role, or to increase your options of employment through gaining awareness of the skills required, the choices you have, the sector generally, and how to prepare a killer CV and shine at interview.

Before we get into the tips and tricks that are going to help you secure your first role, let's briefly cover the skills required for becoming a successful recruitment consultant. I'll also cover a couple of things you don't need, that misguided or ill-informed people often think you do.

Chapter 4

What do you need to become a good consultant?

As you would expect for a job that is communication-based, your written and verbal skills are really important. So, let's start there.

Written Skills

First of all, I think it's really important that we have good written skills. That said, if you're not an academic or if writing is not your area of expertise, that shouldn't hold you back as long as you take the time to use the tools necessary to assist you, like spellcheck. It's important that you read your work back to yourself before anything is published and that you hold your work to a high degree of quality. I am not the strongest literary specialist myself. English wasn't my strongest subject at school and here I am writing a book. So, as long as you put in the effort (and pay your editor well!), then any weakness in your ability is not going to hold you back. I've worked with many people that have had learning difficulties that became great consultants.

Verbal Skills

Naturally, alongside written skills we have verbal skills. These are arguably the more important of the two, since the vast majority of your day you're going to be speaking.

Style of communication

To start with, you need to be a likeable person, or at least be able communicate in a way that people will get on with and relate to you. By that, I don't mean that you need to be the loudest, most confident person in the room. If you ever met me, and I hope one day we can meet, then you'll realise that isn't me. In fact, I cringe at certain social events. So, the main factor in your communication style is that it's relatable to the audience you're speaking to. It's important that you can communicate in a way that has a broad appeal and you can engage with people of both sexes, all ages, levels, races, or religious beliefs. Essentially, the more comfortable you can be, the wider your reach will be, and that can only help.

Advanced communication

You don't need to know long and fancy words but you need to be able to communicate with the people you're dealing with. That means if you're placing teachers, you need to be able to relate and communicate at teacher level. If you're placing CEOs, then your language might need to be a little bit sharper and you might need to have a little bit more knowledge about the terminology that is used at that level. But, ultimately, they're just people, so the key message here is that you need to speak to them on their level. If you're placing nurses and doctors in hospitals, you need to communicate at a level that they would expect. I would always recommend that you communicate at the same level that they do, and that means they don't need you to come in particularly higher or more formal than they do. They don't want you to. Equally, you shouldn't be too relaxed either, and, no matter how comfortable you might get with a candidate or a client, I don't think it's ever necessary to use foul language or profanities. Remember you're a professional!

To summarise, I would expect you to communicate on their level, in a conversational style like you would with a friend over lunch, displaying your industry knowledge that will show you to be an expert in his/her field.

It might vary slightly from industry or sector but that's a good benchmark to work from. So, clear communication is really important and a big part of the job. However, by communication I mean not just the words you say, but how you say it. For example: when you're on the phone often you'll say the right thing but what's said and heard is very different. You need to communicate in a way that the person on the other end of the phone is able to digest the information easily. That means at times you can be hastier and can rattle through it and other times you need to slow down and allow time for them to make a mental note or let their brain process the information.

So, being a good communicator is really important and you need to be aware of how you're communicating, the communication style, and the impact it has on the person on the other end of the phone.

Organisation

Another really important factor you need to be successful recruiter is organisation, especially if you're going into a temp sector where it's fast-paced. These skills are also very important in perm recruitment, but I think especially so in temp sectors. You will need to be very organised and to have fair admin skills. If you're not a natural admin person, as many salespeople are not, don't let this be a challenge to you.

Naturally good salespeople tend to not be good at admin. Just be aware that you're not good at it and have processes in place so you can get over the problems of being unorganised. Again, in temp recruitment that's really important, in particular if you are a three-sixty recruiter because you're likely to have many different applications in your role that you need to apply and deliver every day. I would encourage you to break down your to do list into daily tasks. Don't leave any one thing to be done all on a Friday or all on a Thursday. The best way to stay organised is to break tasks down into smaller chunks.

So, if your target is to place fifty adverts per week, don't place fifty on a Thursday morning. Place ten a day. It's going to be much more convenient and a much easier way to break down the role, and, if for some reason you have to do everything on one day, then do them in one go. Get them done and out of the way in one sitting. Fifty adverts? Bang. Done. Move on. The reason I recommend this is because far too often people have several unfinished tasks on the go, and then nothing gets finished on that day. So, make sure each of your tasks are completed by the end of the day.

Naturally, good organisation skills are really important for the role.

Confidence

Next, in the list of skills required to be a good recruiter is confidence. You need to be a confident person, or at least be able to appear confident. Again, I don't mean you need to be a massive extrovert or the loudest person in the room. That level of confidence isn't useful and actually can become quite annoying. However, you do need to be comfortable in your own skin and be able to communicate with people at different levels at different times, whether you are under pressure or not, whether you're stressed or you're not, and whether you have problems at home or not. This takes composure and confidence.

You need to consistently be confident in your role because people respect confidence and it conveys a level of knowledge, authority, and power.

Drive

Finally, you're going to need a strong drive. This is that unwavering self-belief that ensures you never quit and always get the job done. Too many people quit just as the going gets good because they didn't have enough drive to see it through. I often talk about this as your 'why'. Before I explain more about drive and your why, let's put it into some context.

If you're worthy of a recruitment job and you secure a trainee consultant role, you are probably going to start on a basic salary of around £18-£25k. For the most part, not a terrible salary for an entry level job. However, when you add up all the hours you are going to have to do outside of the contract, the stress, the weekends, and the pressure, then you will come to the realisation that there are easier ways to earn £25k. in fact, anything under £35k. PAs earn this money in London. So, why bother?

Well, you should be coming into recruitment to try to earn at least £60-£80k+. If this is your goal and you can achieve it in year two, then it's very well worth embarking on this journey. However, like I said before, it's not easy. It's brutal, so if you don't have a strong 'why' (why: a reason to make the effort, the gold over the rainbow so to speak), then you will simply end up giving up along the way. And, by the way, "I just want to earn a lot of money" or variations on that might not be enough. Everyone wants to earn more money until they learn what's required to earn more. After that, they quickly find something else to do.

So, those are the main skills and attributes that I look for in a trainee recruiter. To recap, that's good written and verbal skills, good communication skills, being personable and well organised, a strong 'why' or a relentless drive, and the ability to at least appear to be confident whilst you gain your confidence. That's the main tick list for me of the characteristics or skills you need to become a good recruiter and consultant. Some of that you can develop within the role, some of that you're going to need from day one.

Now that you know about the pros and cons of the job and the characteristics required, let's move on and learn more about the different types of recruitment. This will help you interview better, and help you choose the right company to work for. This, in turn, will increase your odds of survival when you start.

Chapter **5**

Recruitment 101

Types of recruitment

Now, before we get into too much detail, I'm only going to cover this topic briefly so you can understand there are differences. This might help you when it comes to your interview process because some interviewers ask about the sectors you're interested in, how recruitment works, or the difference in the sectors. I've covered all of that here but we're just going to cover the general differences so you can be aware of what you're going into.

Sectors

There are recruitment sectors for just about everything you can imagine. In fact, the REC (Recruitment & Employment Confederation) and APSCo (The Association of Professional Staffing Companies) currently list twenty-one or twenty-four different groups, respectively, and there are lots and lots of subgroups and niches within those. So, for pretty much every area of work there's a recruitment sector. That's everything from minimum wage labourers and fruit pickers, right up to the highest senior directors at the biggest global organisations in the world. The levels at which you work are as widespread as you can possibly imagine. There are too many to list here, and which one you end up in will vary for a number of different reasons. It's said that you don't necessarily need to be an expert or have an interest in any field you're going in to. I, for example, made most of my money in the education sector and I am not an academic nor did I have any interest in education. So, I believe that statement to be true. However, what you will need to be successful is to create and develop a level of knowledge for that sector and have some kind of interest in staying with it. This will help you relate to the people in that sector and help you speak as an expert. Those things are definitely going to be an advantage for you.

If you're kind of into IT (and there's plenty of work that sector), for example, you don't need to know about every terminology and every different language applicable, but you should have some kind of interest in those things. If you are speaking to a candidate who has fantastic skills in Flash and he created a piece of work for a client that you genuinely think is good, then that's definitely going to help you sell more effectively.

Temp or Perm?

Moving on from sectors, there are two different styles of recruitment to consider. They are temporary or permanent recruitment. I will now briefly summarise the differences and the way they work.

Perm

If you are a perm recruiter, the process at the start of the appointment will be the same as any other, i.e. find a role, do some candidate work, present some candidates, interview etc. However, you're more likely to have an offer, then a counter-offer, and get an offer again before a deal is agreed to. You are also more likely to have to deal with a notice period than you would as a temp recruiter.

The candidate that you are placing is likely to have one to three months' notice and the candidate will start with the client after the notice period. They will be invoiced a one-off fee which is usually calculated as a percentage of their first-year salary (some are fixed price). This is usually somewhere between ten and twenty five percent of the first-year salary and it is usually invoiced on the placement start date. After the candidate has started, that's the sale. The deal is done. You chalk it up and you move on, looking for a new sale or a separate deal with the same client. You don't tend to have a massive amount of contact with the candidate after that and you won't be able to approach the same candidate again for a different role for a period of time defined in the terms (usually 6-12 months).

Temp

If you are a temp recruiter, then the process up to appointment is very similar. However, there tends to be less of the offer and counter-offer as there is often not a notice period to serve. There are a few differences, however.

 The first is that your candidate, once placed, will do exactly the same job as a permanent appointment or as someone directly employed by the client; however, the way they are paid is different. If the candidate is on a temp contract, they will be paid directly by your agency or their payroll company and not by the company they are working for. They will complete a timesheet at the end of each week and get it signed by their manager (or more often electronically signed off online). Then the agency will use this as authorisation to pay the candidate and invoice the client. The candidate will then work in the assignment for a defined period of time which could be weeks, months or even years. However, when it has finished, the candidate will return to the agency for a new assignment. Hence, good relationships and candidate contact is needed. If you do this well, you will be able to recycle the candidate and place them again and again and continue to earn revenue from them.

Also, due to the nature of the 'temp' market, it tends to be more fast-paced than perm recruitment as a rule. Now, this does depend on the sector you recruit for. However, if you think of some of the reasons why a temp is needed (sickness, high work load, big contract won, short deadline, unfilled post etc.), then you will realise the need for a temp comes around with little notice, which means speed is needed to get the best people in front of the client as quickly as possible before your rivals do.

Which is best?

Of course, there are obvious pros and cons to both.

Perm recruitment tends to be a longer process, temp recruitment tends to be much quicker and fast-paced. In my experience, despite what some will tell you, about the same earning can be achieved (the basic and commission weighting might vary). The choice you will have to make is really just whether you like the hustle and bustle and fast-paced nature of temp recruitment. For example, in education recruitment a consultant can be finding and issuing work to anywhere between five and thirty people in a two-hour window every morning, so you can imagine how fast-paced that kind of recruitment is. It's similar with locums in medical. That's very fast-paced and you need to be organised to succeed at that kind of work.

If you prefer the perm recruitment style, then there is a lot more detail and thought in your work for a longer period. Often candidates are passive in the market, and so you will need to understand what it will take to get the candidate to leave their current role and then you're going to need to hold their hand right through the deal. Equally, you will need to have a much deeper understanding of what the client would like as they are giving you more time to find the perfect candidate. They are going to work for the firm permanently and they are paying one large fee.

So, permanent recruiters tend to do fewer deals for bigger fees and temp recruiters have tens or hundreds of candidates earning them several small fees daily, which is made from the difference between what you pay the candidate and what you charge the client.

Which is right for you depends on you, your personality, your skills, and your attributes.

Three-sixty Consultant vs Candidate / Client Consultants

Finally, the makeup of the role. They are split in a variety of different ways and one of the most common methods is to be a three-sixty recruiter. If you are three-sixty recruiter or a true three-sixty recruiter, then you are likely to be doing every single part of that role yourself. You have full accountability of your particular sector and business. I liken it to running your own small business and with that I mean exactly what I say. It's exactly as if you were the only employee of a small business, so you'll be doing everything from chasing timesheets to processing and creating marketing to cold calls to dealing with candidates to placing adverts to dealing with new applicants to interviews, and everything in between. You do the whole job start to finish. The good part of that means that you are solely accountable for everything, which means you are in control. If you're a control freak like me then that's a fantastic opportunity to have. The negative of that is naturally people aren't good with everything. For example, you might be very strong on sales but might not be very good in your marketing or advertising roles and you need to be able to maintain a good balance of the different jobs to be successful.

If you're not a three-sixty recruiter, then you can be any number of variations of the same role broken up in different ways. For example, in medical they often split the role between the client-facing and candidate-facing (sometimes called one-eighty recruitment). In this set up you would usually see titles like Candidate Consultant or Client Consultant. As you can see, you can split that the role of a three-sixty recruiter up into many different portions depending on the skill required or need for that function. For example, you might also have a Business Development Consultant.

The pros and cons to that are if you're a specialist in an area, then you get to be very well trained and very rehearsed in that particular field. You can be an expert in an area but where the negatives lie is you don't have as much control because it means you have to hand over parts of the deal another person. This means you will need to have really good interpersonal skills and you need to get on with all the people in the different divisions. That can sometimes cause challenges, as the deal might be more important to him than it is you, or vice versa, which naturally could create a problem. So, there are pros and cons to consider.

We have spoken about the different types of sectors you'll be working in. We spoke about temp and perm recruitment and the differences between them, and we spoke about the three-sixty role or any breakdown of that. Now it's time to explain how commission works.

How commission works

First of all, if you've never worked in sales, you should know that the vast majority of recruitment is paid on commission. As a rough rule of thumb, I would expect you to earn at least your basic back in commission. Really, that should be two-fold.

Commission, in its simplest form, means that you get a percentage of the sales you make. The reason you need to know this is because it's going to be a very important factor on how much you can earn. Also, if you don't have a good understanding of how commission works in a business before you move into it, this could be seen as a weakness going into the interview process. When we're interviewing someone for a trainee consultant role often we get to the point where we really like them and can see a lot of good in them. However, we can't hire them as they're what we call 'too green' i.e. they need too much training, or they don't know enough about the job. That decision can come from a number of things (most of which we will address in this book) but it can be something as simple as not even understanding how commission works. In the interest of keeping the book short and punchy I'm not going to go into massive detail but I'm going to give you again a brief overview about how most commission structures work.

Simply, like I said, you get a percentage of your billings. So, that means, for example, if you bill thirty thousand pounds in a month and you're on a ten percent commission structure, you're going to be taking home three thousand pounds. It's important to note there are sometimes deductions made prior to you getting your share (particularly in the bigger firms) and that could be the cost of running your desk or other expenses like the employer's NI. Still, for the most part you're going to get the lion's share of whatever it is you bill.

That's how a basic commission structure works. In this example you get simply ten percent of everything you make.

Threshold and pound zero

Pound zero is a phrase you might hear, and it simply means from the first pound. This might come up in conversation if, for example, the company has a commission structure where there is no threshold. A threshold is a certain level or threshold that needs to be met before you make commission. It's fairly common, so don't be alarmed if you have one. How big it is depends on the desk, industry, company and type of recruitment you are doing. Threshold is considered to be your cost of running a desk. It's usually between three thousand and six thousand pounds – think of it as a barber renting a chair in the barber shop. He has to pay to be there but everything he makes afterwards is his. If you have a threshold, that's the first amount of money that you have to make and you won't earn commission until you are above that figure. Usually you have commission on everything after at the applicable rate.

> ### Commission Structure with Threshold
>
> ### Billings - Threshold x Commission % = £Commission
>
> ### Eg
>
> ### £30,000 - £4,500 x 10% = £2550

If you earn from pound zero then it means exactly that; there is no commission threshold and from the first pound you make for the company you earn a commission percentage.

Often companies will have just a flat fee where you just get a flat % of everything you bill.

> ## Flat Commission Structure or Pound Zero Threshold
>
> ## Billings x Commission % = £ Commission
>
> ## Eg
>
> ## £30,000 x 10% = £3000

Sometimes, you have an increasing scale. This is sometimes referred to as a staircase or sliding commission structure. If you have a staircase scheme, imagine a staircase. Each step represents a new level of billings and with it a new percentage bracket. For example, anything under £5,000 in a month you might receive 5%, anything from £5,001-£10,000 you might receive 7.5% and anything from £10,001 to £15,000 you might get 10% and so on, up to 15%. It's important to pay close attention to your billing on these schemes because if you bill £10,000 you would get 7.5% which is £750, whereas just £1 more in billings would get you into the next commission bracket and bag you £1000. That's £250 more for you with just £1 more for your company. This works the other way too, so if you are on this scheme, track your billings carefully.

Staircase Commission Structure

			15%	< £15,001
		10%	£10,001 - £15,000	
	7.50%	£5,001 - £10,000		
5%	< £5,000			

Some companies will have split billings. This means you might have to split the billings and thus the commission with another consultant and this is common in the one-eighty recruitment sectors for obvious reasons.

Split Commission Structure

Billings x Commission % / 2 = £Commission each

£36,500 x 9% / 2 = £1642.50 each

Finally, some companies use a team bonus. This works similar to the way that tips work in a bar. There is a team target and once it's hit, the bonus is shared out to the consultants on that team. This, for me, is the worst system and one to be avoided. Put simply, in my eyes, systems like these rewards the weak and penalise the strong, which is obviously not a good idea long term, especially if you're planning to be the strongest.

Team Bonus Structure

Billings x Commission % / Number of Consultants = £Commission each

£45,000 x 12% / 5 = £1080 each

Chapter **6**

How to prep your CV for best results.

As this book is intended for those who are early in their recruitment career, I am going to assume you don't have any or much recruitment experience. Once you have a couple of years under your belt, your job searches will take care of themselves. However, as I explained in the introduction, it can be difficult to be seen amongst all of the other applicants unless you make an effort.

In my case, I had significant sales and management experience behind me and yet prior to me adjusting my CV, I didn't secure one single interview.

So, if you are in a similar boat, then use the following advice and take some time to get your CV right.

Put your best foot forward

Ignoring what the template suggests or what you may have read I want you to present your strongest area first. There are typically three main areas to a CV, contact information and statement, education, and experience. Now your contact information has to be present at the top along with your statement, but immediately after that should follow your strongest area. If you are a graduate and you have a strong degree, then offer that right up front. If the opposite is true where you have a stronger work experience but lesser or no education, then lead with the experience. The lesson here is that recruiters are masters at screening CVs and we typically only glance at any one for a few seconds (between five and seven according to a recent study by collingwoodsearch.co.uk) before deciding to read on or move on. So, in putting your best foot first you give yourself a better chance in getting the recruiter to continue to read.

Aside from the usual education and work experience, be sure to include any awards you have won, any league tables, performance listings, promotions, sales or profit figures, % gains or sporting achievements.

This was the major change I made to my CV which I feel made the most difference. If you are a good employee, which I suspect you are, then I'm sure you can think of some things that you have improved or do better than anyone else. If you can, then include them, as recruiters want to know that winning is important to you and that you are used to winning, the same can be said for sales figures, it just shows that you understand numbers and that they mattered enough to record them.

Have a look at the example below as inspiration about how you might demonstrate recruitment skills within a basic retail job.

So rather than

- Asda May 2018 – June 2019
- Senior Cashier

You can have

- ✓ Asda May 2018 – June 2019
- ✓ Part time Cashier May 18 – July 18

- ✓ Senior Cashier July 18 – June 19
- ✓ Processed between 150 -250 customer orders per day
- ✓ Daily sales around £18,000 per day
- ✓ Regularly top 3 producing cashier on my shift
- ✓ Upsold store cards
- ✓ August employee of the month.
- ✓ Trained First Aider
- ✓ Fire Marshall

You can see how a little more thought about your role and achievements can show the recruiter more of what you have to offer and help you stand out amongst similar applicants.

Use keywords

Make sure that your statement or objective is obvious, accurate and keyword sensitive. Immediately after your contact information usually follows a small paragraph which dictates your objective or introduction. This should be short, sharp and snappy, it should describe you, your situation and what you are looking for. This is the part where it should be immediately obvious what you've been doing and what you're looking for. This part should also contain any suitable keywords, such as Trainee Recruitment Consultant for reasons I'll explain shortly.

Substance over style

As we have discussed, recruiters look at hundreds of CVs daily and for just seconds, so unless there is a specific reason why the CV needs to be arty, go for a template that is clean and direct. Most recruiters are not interested in charts or graphics, they just want to find the information they are looking for as quickly as possible. So in the spirit of giving yourself the best chance of being read, make it easy for them with a clean presentation. For the same reason, you should also check that it is consistent throughout, make sure that if you have described the month as

'Dec' in one area that you don't have 'December' written somewhere else. For ease on the eye, all of the sub paragraphs and spaces should all be equal as well. The easiest way to check this is to print the CV and then use a ruler to draw vertical lines down from each of the first words, this will help you see if anything is out of line.

Make sure it's perfect

Check, check, and check again. Make sure the CV you present is grammatically perfect. Use all available tools such as spell check and have a friend read over it before you submit it anywhere. If you have very little experience or qualifications to fall back on, they will be unforgiving to any typos, and rightly so, the same Collingwoodsearch study they found that one spelling or grammar mistake resulted in a CV being thrown away 76% of the time! However, as I have discussed, you don't need to be a perfect wordsmith but you do need to care, and making sure the document is perfect before you submit it is another way you can show that you are on the ball.

Let them come to you

If you are new to this world, or even to the working world you may not realise there are people looking for you right now. It's often easier to make yourself visible to these people than it is for you to try to apply to all of the trainee posts you see. The easy way to do this is to simply upload your CV to all of the major job boards. This is why I said earlier that your CV needs to be keyword sensitive, as when you upload your CV two things will happen. Recruiters who pay for access to those job boards will be able to search for you, and recruiters who have watchdogs set (a watchdog is a simple tool recruiters use to be notified when a candidate who has certain keywords in their CV joins the site) will be notified. This will drive the calls to you.

Just remember to only upload the perfect CV and to make your profile visible in the settings as you set up your accounts. The major UK job boards are listed below.

Reed.co.uk
CVLibary.co.uk
Indeed.co.uk
Monster.co.uk
Jobsite.co.uk

SJ NOTE: *Remember to make sure that your voicemail greeting is suitable!*

Cover Letters

Cover letters are hit and miss for me, I have seen some jobs insist on them and I know recruiters who don't even read them. However I can give you one bit of advice: if you are going to write one, make it personal. It should include the company you are applying for and you should state in detail why you want to work there or what you could bring. In my opinion, a generic cover letter does more damage than good, so if you are using them then make them specific to the job you are applying for.

Chapter **7**

Just call up and invite yourself in

If all else fails, and none of the above methods are working, then this will. Just call up and invite yourself in. Think for a minute; if the internal recruiters or hiring managers at the agencies you want to work at are not seeing the value in your CV, or they can't see how you could be a consultant, or how you would make that transition quickly or easily, then show them.

We have discussed earlier about what characteristics are required to be a good consultant; confidence, comfort on the phone, positive attitude, go-getter etc. If these cannot be easily translated through your CV, resulting in an interview from a job application, then they can be over the phone.

If you are able to call someone you don't know, introduce yourself, build some rapport and close them for an appointment then you have already demonstrated a lot of the skills required to do the job.

I get a few of these approaches every now and then in my main role, and whist some of them are not very confident approaches I always respect the attempt and they get a bit more credibility and a touch further in the process than people who didn't try.

This technique might be especially useful for those of you who have a choppy work history holding several short-term jobs, or those who have only worked in a pub or at fast food chain etc. Whist there is nothing wrong with either of these work histories, it's going to be difficult for the hiring manager to see what skills you can bring and so they will just glaze over your application.

How do you invite yourself in?

Find a company you want to work for, or one you have applied for online, and find out the right contact by using the company mapping / name gathering techniques we discuss later in the book. Then pick up the phone and attempt to speak to them. You should just be able to reach them directly by asking, since they will want to speak to suitable applicants, however, you have the 'beat the gatekeeper' tools at your disposal if you need them (be respectful and sensitive here since you don't want to piss anyone off) Once you have your contact, simply introduce yourself, tell them about you, your background, your experience etc. and invite yourself in.

An example call might go like this:

Good morning Mr Joseph, Thanks for taking the call, you don't know me but my name is Jane Smith, I put through my application for your trainee consultant role last night. I don't expect you have had the time to look through the applications as of yet and so in the spirt of the job I thought I would call up and introduce myself.

After the initial back and forth you can attempt to close by using something like:

> *Listen, I realise my CV might not necessarily jump out at you, hence why I called. Whist I have achieved a lot and grown a huge amount at McDonalds I understand it's probably not going to impress you. I see you're based at Monument, I'm over that way on Tuesday, are you free to grab a coffee so I can introduce myself more formally?*

Now, it's unlikely they will jump straight out and agree to the meeting on that day, they will often push back to the process. If this happens, don't be disheartened. Be respectful to the process, back out and leave it with them.

However, if they promise a call or an invite and it doesn't follow in a sensible timeframe, again do what a recruiter would do: follow up. This is really bold and after this attempt you will likely get the interview/meeting or you will get a firm rejection. If you're thinking that you're not looking for a rejection and you would rather leave it at the maybe stage, it's the same thing. Maybe is no! As we will discuss later in 'take action' it's better to find out what options you have, and this route you will find out exactly where you stand.

It will kill as many leads as it will gain you interviews, and the leads it does kill are only going to be from firms that were at a 'no' anyway and you just didn't know.

Chapter **8**

How to prep and conduct yourself in your first interview

Here we're going to cover some basics, some potential formats on how the interview processes might run, some questions you can and can't ask, and again some information you should have, and research you should do.

Now, obviously I can't cover every possible scenario, and even if I could there are better placed books to read which would advise you on that subject. However, I want to prep you to a) think like a recruiter, and b) understand what the recruiters are thinking and how to show them what they need to see to appoint you.

Prep

Regardless of how quickly your interview came about, and in recruitment they can come about quickly, you need to get yourself interview ready.

Presentation

The first thing is to make sure that you are well presented, and that's a suit with tie for a man, and a dress, skirt or business suit for a woman. Ladies, it's fine to dress to compliment yourself. After all, we want you feeling confident.

However, you shouldn't dress for the club, so no boobs out or tiny skirts.

You should always overdress for your first interview. If you are on the second interview and you know that the dress code is more relaxed, for example, the men don't wear suits but are more chinos and shirts, then it's fine to relax it a little, but not much. In that situation I would lose the tie. However, never lose it at your first interview. You would be staggered at the amount of people that don't get through the first interview because they don't have a tie.

The same is, of course, applicable for women, and it can be worse. If you are dressed too young or have too much on show and you are interviewed by a panel of women, they might have you down as a no before you even get to the interview room. So, for me, it's easy. Overdress until you know better and then only relax it very slightly – why blow it over something simple like what you're wearing?

Punctuality

What can I say? TURN UP ON TIME! For me this one is huge. If you are even a few minutes late, you're almost always going to be a no for me. Sometimes you get people who call ahead or email to say the train was delayed or they had an issue and they will be there late. Frankly, I don't care. There is zero excuse for a late interviewee in my opinion.

So how do you prepare for the unexpected? What if your train is late? Well, that's easy. You get to your interview at least an hour before it starts, you find the building, find the entrance, check you have it right, and then you go and get a coffee while you get your head in the right space and you read through your notes. This way you are not stressed, you are not rushing, and you can calmly walk into the office ten minutes before the booked time.

Research

It's important you know a decent amount about the company you are interviewing at. One, because you want to know what it is you're going in for, and two, because it's almost certainly going to come up in an interview, either in the form of, "What do you know about us?" or "What attracted you to work here?" or some variation of those questions.

So, what do you need to know? Well, at least the basics about how they were formed, what area of expertise they are in, if they've won any industry awards, their size, their different branches etc. Anything positive or unique you can find out about the company and ideally a little more than the opening paragraph on their website homepage. Now, the interviewer won't expect you to know every detail from beginning to end for a trainee position but they will expect you to have made an effort. So, have a look and make some notes.

Outside of the company's website, which will tell you about them, you can find out some really interesting information about a company and in particular what the culture is like, what its staff think of it, the salaries and benefits, and, in some cases even, interview questions on a site called Glassdoor (www.glassdoor.co.uk). it's a really popular company review site. Imagine TripAdvisor for companies. It's kind of the go to feedback site for the employees of companies and businesses. If the company you are interviewing at is listed, you will find out some interesting and useful information. You can also look at Google reviews. However, google reviews are mostly left by customers rather than its consultants and so naturally are often negative. Take them with a pinch of salt. They will give you an indication of what its customers think of the business you will be working in, whereas the Glassdoor reviews are likely to give a true indication of what it's like to work in that company and are usually impartial as the website has some reasonably thorough screening in place. To point out the obvious, and I say this because I have been asked before, if they have negative points you keep that information to yourself, if they have positive points you should feel free to bring that up in an interview as part of your research. For example, "I took a look at your Glassdoor reviews and I noticed that a lot of people where talking about the CPD you offer. That sounds interesting. Could you tell me more about that?"

As you can see doing some homework prior to the interview is not only going to help you interview better, it's going to help you ask better questions and help you decide if it's the kind of company that you want to work for.

It's a two-way interview

Remember, it's a two-way interview. You are there to see if you would like to work for them as much as they are there to decide if you would suit them. A proper career is a marriage and like marriage it should not be entered into lightly. If you are a second-jobber or last-chancer, then you may have already learned this lesson!

Now, clearly you need to get a job offer or at least a second interview to be able to 'choose' them. Thus, your questions should be reserved for the right time in the interview process. This is usually at the back end of the interview and it's fairly standard to be asked, "Do you have any questions for us?" If you do, they should be concise and not run on too long. You don't want them to actually feel like you're interviewing them, just that you're informed and you want to obtain extra information.

I would suggest that the best way to do this is to complete your research prior to the interview and leave yourself about five questions you genuinely would like to know more about or have clarified. Once you have them, you should try to gain the answer or at least a better understanding of the answer throughout the normal interview leaving you two or three to ask at the end.

The reason I want you to be happy with the company you are working for is twofold. One, you are probably more valuable than you might think in the market. You don't have to accept the first or any offer just to "get into" recruitment. Two, where you start your recruitment career is really important. If you get the wrong company, then you're likely to end up back in the job market again within three to six months and that's going to look terrible on your CV.

You need to pick a company that's going to support you and give you the guidance you need for your first twelve months to be able to survive. What you choose to do with your career after that is entirely up to you, but choosing the company with the right training, ethics and culture and has the longevity to see you through and help you get through those first twelve months is really important. And that's where smaller companies can be difficult.

Bigger companies can also be very treacherous as they are likely to have more of a financial view of you rather than a heart view. That's why I personally think medium-sized enterprises are really good for your first role, should you get to find one. They are usually around the £15m-40m mark in annual turnover. The reason for this is because I feel they should be small enough that you are important and that you can make a mark on their business, but not so small that they are so strapped for cash they need you to deliver immediately.

51

Questions you can and should ask

Strong interview questions not only show the interviewer you have an interest in the role; they also highlight what's important to you and can help you show yourself as an intelligent and worthy applicant. The questions below are all considered the norm and should not be a problem to ask. However, like always, you need to choose your moment and tone well. Some can easily come across as invasive if delivered poorly.

- What's the culture of the business?
- What did the top earner make last year?
- What is it that the top earner does that the others don't?
- What does the average biller make?
- How long does it normally take for trainees to reach x level?
- What opportunities are there for progression in the future?
- What training do you offer?
- What's the interview process or next stage?
- What is the recruitment process here?
- Who will I meet in the interview process?
- What time frame does that usually take?
- What commission structure or bonuses do you offer?

Questions you shouldn't ask

Just as the good questions above need to be delivered in the right way and at the right time to avoid any negative impact, the following questions or variations should not be asked, or at least not until the offer stage. If you have a recruiter or an internal recruiter who is setting up the interviews for you, then these are questions you can ask them but not the interviewer directly.

They are all questions you might have and want to ask, but they shouldn't be asked unless in the manner listed above as they indicate the negative aspects of a poor candidate. In short, they present you as a slacker.

- How much holiday do I get?
- How much sick pay do I get?
- What are the hours?
- Do I get a day I can leave early?

Formats

The potential formats that you might be expected to go through could be simple as a telephone interview. It might be the traditional face to face interview with different people over a series of appointments (usually increasing in seniority) or they might do a hot-seat interview where you stay still and various people might swing by for five minutes to twenty minutes with you to get a quick gauge of what you are like.

Sometimes you might have to do role-plays, which can be difficult at the best of time. If you have to do this, it's more important that you rise to the challenge and give it a go without hesitation and with enthusiasm than it is that you get it perfect or right.

Sometimes for the bigger firms you're going to need to complete assessment days. If they do this, they will have you doing all manner of things, from teambuilding to management tasks to presentations or pitches. Again, the main thing here is to get involved, have a go, and be vocal. Recruiters are looking for can-do, confident people.

Finally, you might have to sit a psychometric, personality or aptitude test. If you do, don't be alarmed. They are very good for the most part these days. My advice is to answer with your gut, don't over think them, and don't try to second-guess them. Many of them, including the one we use, have a hidden built in bullshit meter. So, answer honestly and truthfully!

As you have now seen, there are a multitude of routes that you might have to take to secure your job. Remember to be prepared, relax, and be yourself (or at least the best version of yourself!).

If you have managed to ask any of the questions listed above either in your first interview or via the internal recruiter, you should have a gauge of how far you are along the process and if you are on-track in terms of the normal timeframe. Again, this will help you have control and build confidence.

SURVIVE

Timeline: 0-6 months

Objective: To get you through your probation period by avoiding basic mistakes, giving yourself freedom to develop your skills, whist gaining consistency over your performance and increasing the speed at which you develop.

Chapter **9**

The basics

Let's assume you've secured your first recruitment job and you're about to start your first role. Maybe you're already in and in your first week or two. It's important we cover the basics here, the common sense. Nothing here should be ground-breaking to you but, as the saying goes, common sense is not so common.

These basics should be the standard you set for yourself and expect of yourself from day one, regardless of what others are doing around you.

Communication: First of all, your communication; whilst in the workplace, avoid any unnecessary communication that is not appropriate for the workplace. By this I mean keep your swearing to zero or minimal, follow the lead of your seniors around you, and follow their guidance as to what is appropriate for the workplace. It's best to avoid anything lewd, sexual, or racial. Generally speaking, these are good areas to stay away from in any case, but definitely stay away from any of those conversation topics until you settle into the role. Remember this rule, especially if you are at a work party or event where it's easy to relax a little too much and upset someone. I personally have learned this lesson a few times in the past and I have seen plenty of people directly or indirectly fired over it. In this early stage of your recruitment career you don't need any added limelight or pressure. So, keep your communication correct and positive for the workplace.

Time-keeping: Turn up on time without a doubt, always. Again, much like prior to your interview, timekeeping is of vital importance, always. I don't care what the top biller does. You need to be there on time or early every time. That includes your lunch breaks. That includes what time you start at the office and what time you leave. If you go out for a client meeting, you are being watched and judged. This all forms part of the decision about how they view you so don't take the piss. It is not for you to be doing this at that point. Aside from anything else, it shows a terrible work ethic, and you are not in a position where you can do that. Yes, it's true that recruitment isn't fair and there will undoubtedly be people taking the piss and getting away with it, or the top biller might do 'what he wants'. You can too, but later in your career when you are more proven. Once you get 'there' the job is likely to be a lot more relaxed. For now, your work ethic should be to show up on time and be ready to do the job.

Presentation: Recruiters, at least male ones, have a fairly stereotypical image of being massively overdressed and this is not what I mean. A tie bar, pocket square and a money clip are not essentials. Again, look at the cues from the people around you as to what is suitable. Now, I'm not saying you need to look the same. Of course not. Have your own style. What is important is that you are dressed appropriately for the workplace. That means your clothes need to be properly washed, properly pressed, smelling good and you need to look sharp, well groomed, and presentable.

Remember, when you do business face-to-face you are judged on your appearance. It isn't right, but it is also a fact. Something you might not know is that how you're dressed also affects the way that you convey yourself over the phone. A lot of firms have a casual Friday. Do you think that people feel different on this day? If so, then it's not too far of a jump to come to the conclusion that you will sound different, too.

What to wear? If it's appropriate, always wear a suit and I would personally encourage you to wear a tie. If in an interview, then the tie is a must. Regardless of what the culture is believed to be, put a tie on! I can't count the number of times I've seen people fail the interview process because they didn't wear a tie when they should have. It's that simple. So, if in doubt, go overdressed rather than under and definitely avoid anything too relaxed like jeans, leggings, or trainers unless you're absolutely sure that's appropriate and you've been told to do so.

Posture: Believe it or not, your posture is really important as well. If you're slouching at your desk or you put your feet up whilst you're at your desk, what kind of indication does that give to the people around you? Maybe that you're too relaxed, maybe that you're not that bothered, maybe that you are too comfortable and not respectful of the opportunity, or maybe that you're simply not taking it seriously. I'm not saying that you need to be on edge at all times but you should be sitting like you would expect in a work environment, by which I mean back straight and sat properly in your chair. Aside from anything else, good posture will make you more productive and avoid the later back troubles poor posture and a career at a desk can bring.

Present: Be present. That's my next rule. Be present in the job. When I talk of presence I am not talking about attendance. I mean you are mentally present. Avoid anything that is likely to take your presence. The biggest offender is usually your mobile, so I encourage you to put your phone in your drawer until your breaks unless you need it for your clients.

Don't be distracted and be present. When you're speaking on the phone to either a candidate or a client, be engaged to that person on the phone. They should be your only focus. Don't be looking around and seeing what else is going on or looking out the window. It's not only going to help you come across well to your employer, it's also going to help you dial in and be stronger with your sales calls because you're going to be listening intently and actively taking part in the conversation rather than just going along with it.

B+: I want people around me that are can-do. I want people that believe that it is possible, and I want people to think they can. It's really important. If you're a naturally negative person or you have a negative stance given to you by your friends or family, get rid of it now. It's going to seriously impede you in recruitment. Remember to always be positive, have a can-do attitude and always do what's possible. It's going to be really visible in the way you convey yourself, so If that is not naturally how you are, before you visit the office each day get yourself in the right mental state and be present in the work you're about to do.

Telephobia: I'm going to touch on the final thing which is something someone clever coined as a telephobe; a person who is scared of the phone.

I'll let you in on a secret here. If you're scared of the phone, guess what? Most of us are to some degree, at least to begin with. I can tell you that not many people genuinely enjoy cold, outbound sales calls and not many people enjoy rejection. Rejection is pain and we are fight or flight creatures, so in the face of pain we are programmed to get out. It's just not something that we're programmed to enjoy.

That said, you are going to have to dial the phone, and a lot. So, if you want to make the money that you set out to make it in this job, you're going to have to be able to get comfortable on phone. Get used to it and do it quickly. The easiest way to do this is 'rip the Band-Aid off' – just get on with it and do it. So, if you're given any task in the early days, take any and every opportunity to make outbound calls whether they are to candidates or clients and make the calls you don't want to make as often as you can.

Telephobia is something that your employer will spot easily enough. If you are so scared of the phone that you don't think you can push through, then the job simply isn't for you. If you find yourself busying yourself with lots of long emails or picking up more inbound calls than everyone else, you are finding reasons not to be making outbound calls and your employer will spot this. If you're not comfortable on the phone but you can get over it, if the end justifies the means and you want to get used to it, the easiest way to get used to it is just to push through the pain and get it done.

Just remember this: What's the worst that can happen? There is nothing that can happen on that phone that is worthy of the worry it's causing you. The absolute worst thing that can happen, your maximum exposure, is that they hang up or swear at you. Would that really be that bad? You could handle that, right? If it's not that bothering you, then it will be the fear of getting it wrong and looking stupid in front of everyone else. If this is the issue that's got you stalling, then let me tell you your employer is never going to think negatively of you because you made the sales call and it went badly, especially not in the early weeks/months. What's far more important is that you're making the calls so they can teach you and you can learn to make better ones.

If you end up with any level of untreated telephobia, you will end up making fewer and fewer calls which slows your rate of progression and limits your opportunity to put deals together. This has an effect on sales and, as a result, you build more pressure on yourself to have to succeed quicker before you are asked to leave. So, as you might have guessed, it's best to get on top of it quickly, or simply quit if you can't do it.

Over-preparers: Over-preparing is an early stage of telephobia. What tends to happen is that the consultant wants to spend time analysing every possible angle or scenario about how the call might go and plan the 'perfect' call.

Now, I don't want you dialling the call blindly. I want you to have an idea of where you want it to go and how you want to get there. What you can't do is over-prepare. This is for two simple but fundamental reasons.

The obvious one is it's not time effective. Imagine you spend time to plan the call as described above and you finally get yourself in the place where you're ready to make the call. Then you ring them, "Hi, is 'Name' there?" and the contact will respond "Hello, she's not home. She's on holiday and will back in two weeks." The result you just wasted twenty minutes preparing for a call that didn't happen.

The second reason that you can't over-prepare is because calls just don't go like you would imagine. The 'perfect call' isn't crafted out on paper before you ring, like the route on a sat nav. It's more of a general direction that you sail using the available winds at the time, like you would on a sailing ship.

So, be sufficiently prepared that you can make a good call if it connects, but not so prepared that it stops you from reaching a meaningful number of clients or candidates.

That's the basics covered now, so if you have your first role and you are following the guidelines above, there should be no reason for you to be under any negative spotlight now, bar perhaps for your performance, which we will cover in Thrive.

Chapter **10**

Survival of the fittest

In terms of a timeline, you are probably in the 3-9 months period by now. You probably have made a few basic placements, got a couple of early accounts on board, and you're probably feeling okay. You should be starting to move in the right direction if you're following the book and you're putting in the work that's required.

Let me introduce you to my theory of the survival of the fittest.

What you will often find when you are in recruitment is they're likely to have hired trainees and they're often hired in bulk; this means you'll often start amongst other trainee consultants that either started on the day you started or thereabout (remember my story from the start?).

If this is the case, your mission should be to become the most competent person in the group. If you've used the book as a guide so far, and you've applied the things we have discussed, you should be one of the better of your group. If you find yourself as the most competent person in your group, then you simply need to outlast your competition.

It's a bit of an odd tactic to be almost 'the best of the worst' but hear me out. If you are the most reliable, most

65

trustworthy, and the most skilled amongst your junior colleagues, and you're in an industry where people typically don't last very long, then by default you're likely to be given accounts that they picked up.

You see, most people gain a client or two throughout their recruitment career, even if it's under six months. When they depart the business, somebody needs to deal with those clients. Your natural thought might be that the top biller or the manager would take them; however, you will often find that the big biller or the highest billers have long standing accounts and they have lots of workload already by dealing with them. Thus, they're not going to be very interested by an account that's a very small-billing or very green accounts.

Put simply, they will often come to the conclusion that the account will require too much work for too little return for them. They can simply put the same work into their big accounts for more in return.

But for you, as a trainee recruiter or as a recent starter, a new account is going to be lovely news. You will have the time and effort to give it the attention it needs to open it up fully and grow the account. So, just by surviving longer than your colleagues or being more competent than them, you'll often find that you are the first choice when it comes to dealing with new accounts that somebody else has brought on and left. This is another way to thicken your arsenal of accounts and give yourself more rope to keep going while you learn.

Later on, as you move towards the middle of the sales table and you have bigger or more reliable accounts, you might choose to knock one of your accounts off or give them to a junior consultant. However, in the early days you need to take anything you can to increase your billings and keep the pressure off you.

Cheeky pint?

Along with my survival of the fittest method of being the most competent person in your group, another way you can hedge your bets and increase your chances of picking up more accounts is to socialise. Lots of you probably got into recruitment because it is a social job, and hopefully you did, because there is a lot to be had from the social side of the business, especially when times are tough. You should regularly enjoy a social pint, or whatever your chosen poison is, at the end of the week or perhaps the end of each evening. This is especially important if your seniors, managers or directors are present and even more so if they're not there that often.

Now, let me be clear; I absolutely despise ass-licking or brown-nosing and I do not encourage you to do that at any time. But, recruitment is a social game, so if there is an opportunity to take a drink with a director or one of the senior billers or managers, spend some time with them and get to know them on a personal level whilst they get to know you, this is going to help you when it comes to making those difficult decisions about who gets what accounts or who gets fired and who doesn't.

I am not suggesting you want to be keeping your job just because you are liked or that you're the best of the worst even if that was possible, you wouldn't earn any money anyway. Still, to highlight a point I have made a couple of times already, in your first three to six months of your career if you are not smashing your targets, hedging your bets is going to help. And if you can make sure, again, that you're a person that people enjoy being around, you are good for the office and you add value in other ways aside from your billings, then you're going to be chosen to survive longer than someone that isn't liked or useful. So, it's very important that you take the time to socialise within the respectable boundaries of the business.

Warning: Don't go over the mark and end up getting so smashed that you can't go into work the next day or that you roll in half-drunk or stinking of booze. But if you can enjoy a casual pint or a relaxed drink on a Friday just to settle that balance and to keep yourself in the right circles, then I would actively encourage you to do so.

Chapter **11**

The spiral effect and how to ride it

Most of what I learned in recruitment, and is contained within this book, has either come from my seniors, managers, the people I have worked with and for, combined with all the things I've read. But the spiral effect I'm very proud of because it's one of my very own analogies. I use it all the time and I think it's so true.

What is the spiral effect?

The spiral effect is really simple. If you think of a spiral shape like a tornado and then you think of another tornado directly on top of it upside down, you end up with like a pyramid shape, a spiral-shaped diamond made up of one, long looping line. Once you have the image of the shape in your head, you need to think of the spiral as your mojo. If you then think of a solitary bead on the spiral like you would have on an abacus, the bead is always either going up or down. It's never standing still. The bead represents your 'live' energy or outlook, with either end being a pole like the positive and negative poles of the north and south pole or the fields on a magnet.

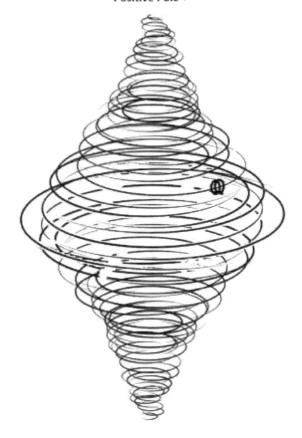

Peak Positive Energy

Positive Pole +

Negative Pole -

Peak Negative State

What tends to happen is you don't stay in the same place very long. If you think about the bead as your emotional state, it's moving towards the positive end when your well-being is good, you feel confidence within the job, you're performing well against targets, you're healthy and your personal relationships are good etc. And in this state you are gently rotating and climbing towards the top of this spiral.

If you think of the flip side of that, it is being in a negative state. For example when you are passively job seeking because you hate the job you are doing, everyone you placed either falls out or the deals don't go through, your earnings are behind and money worries are creeping in, you have a sick family member, things at home are difficult, one thing after another is piling up on you, and you're having a general lack of success, then you're in a negative state. You're going downwards on the spiral.

There's a bit of a compound effect that applies to the spiral when you're on the negative side; when things are going bad, usually more things go bad on top of that. You accelerate faster and faster towards the pit, the oblivion, the bottom of the spiral (what is often called rock bottom).

Naturally, all poles have an opposite and the same laws apply. The compound effect also applies to the positive side only what happens on the other end is when you are doing well you tend to continue to perform better. That's why most sales companies will say as soon as you made a good sale and you've closed the deal, don't rest on your laurels. Get straight on the phone and get going again. It's because the positive energy in your voice, in your tone, in the way you carry yourself is likely to be carried

What to do when you become aware of the spiral

The first thing to do with the spiral effect is be aware of it. When you find yourself in an upward spiral, and you're like King Midas where everything you touch turns to gold, capitalise on it! Compound what's going good for you, deliver as much as you can at a higher rate, and force that bead up to the top of that spiral as fast as humanly possible, grabbing all the commission you can on the way. This, my friends, is when records get broken.

You are not likely to need too much encouragement on that side of things because that tends to happen naturally to people. The thing that you can do is be aware that nothing lasts forever, so you really should maximise the opportunity while it's there. Sooner or later you get a bad blow and things start to go the other way. It might be that a deal you made drops out, that a good deal doesn't pay, or something completely out of your control, but your positive streak is up. The bead is moving.

As I have covered, the positive stuff tends to take care of itself; however, what you will need be aware of, especially in your first three to six months, is the negative side. When you're going downwards or when you are in a downhill struggle, you're going the opposite way on the spiral and there is no easy way out of it. If you're on a bad luck streak or you're in a bad role and everything is going wrong, you are not going to be able to change the outcome very easily. This is often when people leave the sector and become just another recruitment statistic. They walk away muttering something like, "I gave it my all, but it wasn't for me."

Well, that doesn't have to be the case. Now, you can't stop and get off the spiral. We are metaphorically on it forever. What we can do though, is to learn to manage it and play the game better. You can start by being aware of it, and that should change your actions, work rate and perception of what's happening. Once you can do this, you can start to reduce the speed of the direction, slowing the bead going downwards and slowly bringing it back the opposite way.

It might even mean that one good call or one good deal that slows the bead up or stops it or starts it moving in the other way. Then you need to force it with a snowball effect. You're going to need to start stacking your ups and stacking your positive work to start to move the bead in the other direction until you get a bit of success, followed by a bit more and so on. Then the bead starts to move up the spiral, moving towards the top and creating a positive spiral effect.

Now this all really links to 'state management', a fascinating topic, and one I would recommend you research further. Still, it's a nice visual tool I use with my trainee consultants to illustrate mood and how you can control it and use it to your advantage. What happens once you get experienced is that you learn to manage outcomes better, plan further ahead and become less dependent on one or two outcomes. This helps all of this become less relevant. However, if you have just started in recruitment, then I'm sure you will relate to my trusty spiral!

Chapter **12**

The Water Cooler Effect

Be careful about the company you keep in recruitment.

"The Watercooler Effect" is a study and the title of an American book by the author Nicholas Di Fonzo. It looked at people who gathered around the water cooler and why we spread rumours, why we believe them, and how they affect our behaviour. Now, whilst we don't have many water coolers anymore, the scenario is still present in every recruitment office.

Often, the people who spend an abnormal amount of time in these places are not at their desk doing what they should be because they tend to be people who have a victim mentality, people that are in a negative mindset or people who are disengaged.

I mentioned in the previous chapter about the spiral effect and the need to be aware of your position on it and control your direction. As discussed previously, a lot of your direction of travel comes from your outlook, mindset and state, so naturally you will want to stay well clear of these people at all costs. They're likely to pull you in a negative direction.

Hopefully, you're a positive person and, if you're not, hopefully you're working on becoming more positive as this is

75

going to be a factor as to whether you are successful in recruitment. So, stay away from the negative people.

Very negative or disengaged people tend to take excessive smoking breaks or spend too much time around the water cooler or kitchen. Once you've spotted a "negative Nancy" or a "mood hoover", make sure you stay well away from them and choose your company carefully.

You should try to be in the company of the top billers, the top producers or the management team, not from an ass-licking point of view, but from a point of view that they're likely to have a positive mentality that is going to help benefit both your career and personal life, as opposed to a negative mentality that will hold you back.

Now, I am not saying that if you smoke you are negative or if you like a brew you must be disengaged; however, you will often find that people that fall into those groups look for places to hang out and burn productivity. Watch out for them!

Be careful where you get your advice

It always amazes me to see that trainee recruiters or junior recruiters tend to ask other low billers for advice. I guess that comes because the senior managers, top billers or the directors tend to be more time-precious and less approachable. However, you have to remember what you're doing there; you're asking someone who doesn't know much about the job to give advice to someone who doesn't know anything about the job. Does that sound like a sane choice?

What do you think the quality of the information is going to be like? Now, sadly they're going to be very helpful. They're going to be all guns blazing wanting to help you, so they'll probably give you a lot of advice and they'll probably spend a lot of time with you. But what you will find is that the advice is simply not right; after all, if it was right, they would be more successful themselves.

Make sure you take your advice from the people who are in the position you aspire to be in. On that note, if you are given advice, or rather direction, as it should be called, then apply it quickly and consistently. After all, how long do you think the advice tap will be on if you always ask but never do? That is the exact definition of an 'ask hole'!

ask·hole

[ask hōl] *noun*

a person who constantly asks for your advice, yet always does the opposite of what you told them

In summary, be careful about the water cooler effect, where you find your influences, and the advice that you are given.

THRIVE

Time: 6-12 months +

Objective: To make the most of this career path you have chosen, to not only increase your billings, but to start to climb your way towards top biller status by increasing your efficiency, your meaningful contact, improving your control in conversations, and working on advanced tones.

Now we get to the nitty-gritty of this book.

If you have a job already in recruitment and you're in a company that seems to be right for you, you may think the Secure part of the book was of little value to you. Equally, if you are getting towards the end of your probation and you know you have done enough to pass, you may come to the conclusion that, although there were some good points, most of what you read in Survive was common sense. You might think that this has been a waste of money so far, but, believe me, the next few chapters are golden. They really are my truest and most used techniques and these are the techniques that I train and preach every day. You should read these techniques daily, research them further, and apply them immediately.

Take notes on this section in the book because this really is the stuff that will make you thousands, if not hundreds of thousands, of pounds in your career.

So, stop being negative and keep reading, you cheapskate!

Chapter **13**

Tone and vocabulary

Tone and vocabulary both deserve a book on their own. They're subjects that are infinitely more complicated and complex than you need to know at this point in your career, so I will just lead with the introduction of the point.

It is vital you understand more about these subjects if you are to truly become a master in your craft, and becoming a master of your craft is what we want from the Thrive section of the book. What you need to understand is that what we're doing here as salespeople is an art. It's something that can be, and should be, practiced and refined over a period of years. Top producers or top billers in any field are top billers for a reason. They refine their craft to such a level that they can expect and predict results.

Tone and vocabulary basics

When you're speaking, it's really important to understand that the words that you use, the way that you say them, your tone, and your pace have an impact. Some words mean more than others. Some words have negative connotations and some words have positive connotations. The same can be said for pace, and a slower pace generally holds more authority than a faster pace. Likewise with pitch. A lower pitch pulls rank over a higher pitch, and so once you are over your telephobia and you are comfortable on the phone, it's time to start applying some craft to your work. Aside from tone, pace and your choice of vocabulary, some words have an effect on the conversation at a subconscious level. For example, some words are minimisers, some words are closers, some words are leading, and some words have a much bigger impact than is first thought. So, you need to apply some thought around not only what you say, but HOW you say it.

Example:

Think of a stereotypical telephone salesperson. Usually, they're high-pitched and over-enthusiastic over the phone, and that instantly loses credibility. I am sure you can think of a time you had a PPI call or a Trip or Fall claim call. They open the call with, "Good evening, is this Stephen?" (said in an overly enthusiastic fast and upbeat tone). You instinctively know it's a sales call before another word is said and you have switched off. How can that be the case? After all, all they did was ask if it was the right person. It's because faster than you can even think about it in your conscious mind, your subconscious has processed the words, tone, pace and pitch against what it knows and it instantly draws the conclusion that the call will be a waste of your time and sends a message from your brain to your speech to formulate the best words to instantly get rid of the caller. That's tone working against you.

Now, think of the other end of the spectrum; people in authority, for example, a judge, a doctor or a police officer. They will almost always speak slowly and calmly in a deeper tone. Because we respect these people and we naturally think that what they have to say needs to be noted, we pay attention.

Imagine the same words as above said in the tone of a police officer. Slow, deep, calm but authoritative. "Good evening, is this, Stephen?" Our minds instantly race and we instinctively answer quickly, "yes," in a curious or even concerned tone! We are thinking, "Oh god, what has happened? Is everything okay?"

Exactly the same words have a profoundly different impact on our subconscious and generate a different reaction. That's tone working for you.

It's worth noting that people of authority or value rarely speak quickly, and if you have met any significantly wealthy or powerful people, such as the CEO of a large company, you will be able to confirm this. That is because the words that they're using have impact and people naturally will listen, so there is no need for them to rattle off a hundred words per minute.

Equally, you may have heard a very nervous person make a presentation or a speech. They tend to naturally end up speaking really fast and speak in an ever-increasing pitch as the nerves build.

In summary, it's important for you to choose the right tone when you speak if you are going to portray the right 'image' over the phone. After all, over the phone we can be anyone we want to be.

It's worth noting if you are female or a male with a naturally high-pitched voice, it's worth consciously lowering your pitch when you make your calls, at least until you have rapport built with your contact.

Pace

It's also worth being very conscious and aware of the pace of your words, especially when you come under fire in a call. Let's say you have beat the gatekeeper (more on this later in the book). You have got your DM (decision maker) on the phone and you have opened well, all at a calm, deep authoritative tone, and at a good pace. All is well.

However, you meet a problem and you are challenged by a rejection you are not prepared for. Your confidence drops a little, but you respond. Your pace and tone increase just a little, but you push on. Following that you really hit a nerve and now the DM has grown angry. You try to calm them down but naturally as you do so, the tone and pitch increase again. You will find that if the call lasts much longer you will end up so high and so fast the dogs will start barking. The point I'm making here is that when people are under threat, we all naturally increase our pace and tone, which, as we now know, costs credibility. So, get used to opening well, and watch your tone and pace, especially if you are under fire as this is where it's likely to rise.

Dinner's ready

If you think back as a child, you can remember your younger self happily playing upstairs when your mum shouts your name. I am sure you can starkly remember the difference in the tones of when she calls your name to tell you dinner is ready, and when she calls your name after she has just discovered that you broke her favourite ornament!

You can see how saying the same word but applying a different tone can have a very different meaning.

Tone, pace, and vocabulary are very, very important.

As I said, this is an area you should do further research and apply your knowledge as you gain more experience.

In summary: -

Pace: Slow it down, stay calm, and don't let them rush you.

Pitch: Lower is better. Avoid getting higher if your pace increases.

Tone: Aside from the words you are saying, what is the tone you are saying them in suggesting?

Does it confirm the word or is it conflicting against your words? This is especially important if you have an upward inflection as this is likely to make you sound unsure, even if you're sure.

Vocabulary: What does the word mean? Be careful about what you say. You might be doing more damage than you think. For example, we all know the trick retailers use to reduce the perceived value of an item. When it's described as "just 12.99 per month", they are trying to reduce the figure. Great choice of words, but what happens when you use the same trick and you describe your call as "just a quick call"? Exactly the same. You reduce the value, i.e. you set their subconscious off thinking, "Oh god, it's a sales call. Thankfully he said it's quick so he will go soon and I can get on with my day!"

Not the way you want to start your call.

I believe passionately in the power of this in effective telephone calls, so I would suggest you research more about it. One book I can recommend in particular is Jordan Belfort's book "Way of the Wolf". It's a fantastic book about selling and has a large chunk dedicated tone and vocabulary. It goes into massive detail in that particular book and it helped me shape my sales pitches.

"Pick up the god damn phone."

Leading on from "The Wolf of Wall Street" the famous line from the movie "pick up the god damn phone" is never truer than in recruitment. There's no way you're going to make any money other than picking up the phone, and yet I see time and time again where consultants new and old find countless reasons to 'busy' themselves with other actions. This is counterproductive.

Even in the case that you get an email sent, for example, pick up the phone. See if you can answer the email in a call. You can still follow that up with email information if it's required, but you should never miss an opportunity to speak to a DM. It's an opportunity to gather information as well as build rapport.

As you get busier, you will feel the need to call less, telling yourself lies like 'I'm passed that' or 'I'm glad I don't have to do that stuff anymore'. This is simply not true. We all need to be on the phone as much as possible. It's simply where our real work is done and it will help you avoid the yo-yo effect we discuss later.

It would be the same as a football coach trying to train his team by getting them to watch videos, discuss strategy, and do role play exercises in a boardroom without getting out there on the field. Like with everything in life, if you want to beat the game and win, you have to roll up your sleeves and get busy. So, stop making excuses for yourself about the other things you are doing, or how it's different for you or your clients.

Get busy, pick up the god damn phone!

Chapter **14**

Tips and tricks of the trade

Now that we are firmly in the last third of the book, I'm going to share with you my tried and tested tips and tricks that have been in my "recruiter's toolkit" for years now. We are going to learn how to map a company/name gather and the most important skill of all – the lost art of "how to beat the gatekeeper". (this section is worth the cost of the book alone!).

Strap yourself in and read carefully. The tips that follow, if applied correctly, will make the difference between how many decision makers we reach and how often which <u>will</u> directly impact your bottom line. This is where the true value of the book lies.

Name gathering / company mapping

What is name gathering and company mapping?

Well name gathering is as simple as it sounds. It is the process of gathering the names of the relevant people in the company. Company mapping is where we draw a mental picture of who they are, what responsibilities they have, and who they report to. This very simply ensures we are speaking to the right people who are responsible for the areas we need, i.e. hiring managers and their superiors. Remember anyone other than the hiring manager will only have the power to say "no" and never "yes" regardless of how good your pitch is because they simply don't have the authority to say yes, whereas the hiring manager or their superiors can, and will, say yes if what you're offering is of value. To avoid wasting our time and theirs, we need to ensure that we are pitching at the right level, and this is the reason we need to take the time to go through the process.

How to name gather or company map

There are a number of ways you can name gather or company map and their effectiveness and cost vary depending on your sector. People often use LinkedIn, one of the sophisticated products on the market, but the cheapest, simplest and, in my eyes, the quickest way is to just pick up the phone and ask.

As you have surely noticed by now, I am an old-school recruiter and I believe firmly that the phone should always be in your hand, so it's not surprising to see that I favour this route. The simplest and easiest way to do name gathering on the phone is to ring through the receptionist or the relevant department and ask a direct question. "Good morning. Who is the business manager for x department?"

Remember, don't beat around the bush and be direct. Ask a direct question and you will get a direct answer most of the time. So, keep it as simple as the example above and avoid things like,

"I wonder if you can help me. I'm looking to send some information to the x department and I wanted to find out who...."

Now, you may have found that you have done this and it worked for you, and, to be honest, if it's working for you, then roll with it. However, over a period of time you will have more success with the first example for two reasons. 1. You don't declare your hand too early and you eliminate the need for the receptionist's input with regards to how useful your information is to the DM, and 2. Receptionists are, by their very nature, used to taking direction. So, if you approach them that way and don't show any weakness, they will just buckle and give you the answer you want.

Remember, as with all these techniques, they are not a silver bullet. You can't just try it and it will work every time. Rather, they are more like playing poker with technique. Once you know how to play poker, even if you get good at it, you will still lose some hands and some games. The key in poker, much like in recruitment, is to increase your hit rate and win more than you lose.

Once you have one name, it's very easy to use your knowledge of that person to find the rest of the relevant people around him or her, i.e. who they report to. When you get him you can quickly and easily ask, "Who do you report to?", "Who reports to you?", or as you can make a suggestion (even if it's wrong) and add validity to your presence by questioning, e.g., "So, you must be Dave's boss then."

So, you can see how, by using the techniques listed above, you will quickly be able to find out who you need to speak to, and who has what responsibility within the company or organisation you are targeting.

Gaining direct emails

Once you have the name, the next part is to start to reach them, and whilst we 100% definitely want to get them on the phone, this can take some time. So, since we want to start marketing to them ASAP, the quickest and easiest way to get our info in front of them is to pop them an email.

91

It's important to note that we want a direct email, i.e. a work email address that will reach your DM specifically, not a general or mailbox account. Mailbox accounts usually start payroll@, Enquires@, HR@ info@ contact@ etc. These mailbox accounts are rarely manned, and even if they are, they often go to multiple people which means it's nobody's responsibility to man them. Thus, your message will get lost. This is also a reason why receptionists will happily give it to you as they know you will never reach the DM. Put simply, we don't want these emails. We want the direct one.

Remember, the action of sending the email is only of value to you if it is read. A thousand emails sent is worth less than one email read.

What you will find is once you have one direct email, the entire company's emails will be set up in the same format, so you can simply guess the rest with a reasonable degree of accuracy. This is because the email structure is usually set up by the IT department and the IT department doesn't have protecting the DM's time in mind when they create them. IT people are usually people of structure and process and they want to create a lot of email addresses in a simple functional format.

Once you have secured one email, and you can almost definitely find at least one on the internet, you can find the format and work the rest out.

The most common formats are:

initial.lastname@Companyname.com
lastnameinital@Companyname.com
firstname.lastname@companyname.com

Once you found that magic first one and you know the first and last name of the people you need to reach, then you can go ahead and fill up your database for marketing purposes with everyone and anyone relevant.

So, get a direct email and then hack the rest.

NB: If the business is on lock down and very often targeted you might have trouble even getting the first one. In that extreme example, I would simply send a test email to all 6-7 options and put a delivery receipt on the email. You will then get 6 bounce backs saying, "undeliverable" and one saying, "delivered". You will then have the information you need to start.

Chapter **15**

How to beat the gatekeeper: Introduction

So, now you're in your recruitment. You're fairly comfortable in the basics, you know what you should and shouldn't do on a daily basis, and you are fairly knowledgeable about your sector. You're going to learn, if you haven't already, that the next biggest challenge you're going to have to face, and what is probably the last big hurdle, is how to beat the pesky gatekeeper.

If you're not in recruitment yet and you don't know what a gatekeeper is, the gatekeeper is the person that's between whoever picks up the phone and the person you want to speak to. It's usually a receptionist or a PA.

If you are still quite naive or you are new to client work or business development, this might be alien to you. This is the bit that they don't tell you about in your interview or in the job description, and it is a true art.

Arguably, making the sales call is the easy bit. Actually getting someone of influence on the phone (a DM) to hear your call is much more difficult.

If that naive person I described above is you, then you probably have a rose-tinted view of what the challenging parts of the role are and you had no idea that this was even going to be an issue. Well, let me tell you that even if you have the most fantastic company, the perfect candidate and you can make your client tens of thousands of pounds, they are still going to instantly brand you as a nuisance. They will not put you through to the DM.

So, this is an important skill to learn as your ability to beat the gatekeeper and regularly get your contact on the phone plays a huge role in how much you can thrive.

It's also worth noting that high-level DMs don't actually get pitched to that often, as their receptionists and PAs usually do a great job in keeping salespeople out. This means that they will often be less rude, sharp, or challenging than the gatekeepers that protect them. This makes the sale fairly easy, assuming you have something useful to sell. Remember, the biggest clients and the highest-level DMs have the best gatekeepers. So, like anything in life, if you want to get the good, you are going to have to graft for it. In some cases, they might have two or three gatekeepers to stop you from getting your DM on the phone. Sometimes, even getting to the DM's PA is an effort, where the receptionist screens your call to the PA before you can even attempt to get around them.

The most challenging part of your role from here on out is your ability to beat the gatekeeper consistently.

Low-hanging fruit

If you think logically, like I do you, might already be thinking, "You said that the biggest clients have the hardest to reach DMs. So, why would I try them? I'm doing okay already working at the middle or bottom of the food chain and there are easy deals here. Is it worth the effort?"

Well, if you are thinking that, I wouldn't blame you. The answer is simple, but before I answer, let me lead you with a thought.

Here follows a thought that was presented to me by the late, great Chet Holmes, and it's one of the reasons why I got into recruitment or sales in the first place!

"If you can master the art of getting DMs on the phone, you are usually just one or two people away from the richest or most powerful men and women in the world!"

In fact, if you don't know Chet Holmes, do some research on him. Again, some of his material really helped me in my early days, but what's cool about him is that after he had made his fortune in sales (he worked for the billionaire Charlie Munger, currently worth around 1.7b USD), he wrote a screen play and actually started cold calling Hollywood production companies to get it made into a movie. SPOILER ALERT! Long story short, after some work on the phone he actually managed to pitch his screenplay to Warner Brothers and they bought the movie!

How cool is that?

So, to answer the question above, "Why should I not just focus on the low hanging fruit? Why should I bother with the big DMS?", well, aside from the fact that the biggest and highest DMs hold the keys to the most valuable clients, which if gained will result in top-producer status for you, it's also a vital skill to learn, both for business and for personal reasons (which I'll talk about later in the book).

Chapter **16**

How to beat the gatekeeper: Mindset, approach, and theory

As with a lot of this book, 'Your Guide to the First 12 Months in Recruitment', I'm going to just touch on the topic here and give you my top strategies but I suggest you do more research on this. See any speaker you can on the subject, watch any YouTube videos you can find (mine are coming soon!), read any articles or books you can get, and practice this at every opportunity you can find. If you master these skills, then nothing can stop you.

Now, how hard it will be and how long it will take depends on you, but remember one rule; it's the gatekeeper that you need to get passed, not pitch. As the saying goes, "Don't pitch the bitch." The good news here is that, usually, the tougher the gatekeeper is, the easier the contact is to sell to, and the more there is at stake.

Let's get started

Before we talk about the actual techniques used to get the DM on the phone, I want to speak about the 'state' or 'mindset' we need to have before we even pick up the phone. As this is just as important as what you say and how you are going to speak as we have already learned.

Desire – Whatever it takes

When it comes to getting a DM or a contact on the phone, your desire is really important. You have to really want to reach that person. Remember, you have to work with a timeframe that works for them, not you. This means that if you find out that your best window is Sunday at 7.00p.m., then you set a reminder, fire up your laptop and give it a shot. You can't expect to get your DM in the standard routine call slots that work for you. Of course, you can try and, in a lot of cases, you will get them, but if you really want to catch them, you will have to do whatever it takes, whenever it takes!

That could also mean ringing first thing in the morning at 5.30a.m., it might mean ringing last thing at night at 7.30p.m., it might mean ringing the mobile, or ringing the direct dial. You're going to need to have a strong desire to be able to get that person and that needs to remain true and consistent; in other words, you can't just give it a go and if it doesn't work, quit. This simply won't work, and is probably what you have been doing up until this point.

Persistence is key

The second thing to consider is persistence. I have some DMs that took me six months of trying my best stuff three to five times a day to reach. Others I did the same for a year and still didn't get them!

Even if you have tried everything you can think of, you must keep pushing. Sometimes the contact just picks up the phone because the receptionist is not there that day, the receptionist is sick and they have a temp in, or you've worn her down and she puts you through, or you might simply have caught her in a particularly strong way or in a great mood and for some reason today she just transferred you.

The point is that persistence is key. If you want your DM and you keep trying you WILL get them in time.

> **SJ NOTE:** *You will be relieved to know that the above examples are extreme. In most cases, with the right techniques, you will get your DM reasonably quickly, usually in around 2-3 well timed and intelligent attempts.*
>
> *You must be ready to pitch at any time*

Another common failing is that we put so much effort into beating the gatekeeper that we don't put enough effort into preparing for the words we're about to say after we get the DM. Therefore, we fluff our one chance, and, as you know, we rarely get a second.

Always be ready to pitch and always assume your call will be connected. I can't tell you the amount of times I have seen someone work for months to reach a DM only to be connected and completely fuck it up because they hadn't expected to reach him. They often mutter something under their breath like "I didn't think he would pick up", well why did you ring him then!

Do you really think you are going to get back in front of them a second time?

Be prepared. Be ready to pitch at any time.

Confidence and belonging

The next part comes with your confidence. You are going to need to convey yourself as confident on the phone (even if you're not), and you're going to need to do so in a way that the receptionist believes you belong in that space.

Whoever you are about to speak to will have some power because they should have power over the buying. That might be a top-level executive, or it might be mid-level manager, but they have buying power, and people with power tend to speak to people of power. For this reason, you will need to convey confidence in a direct and authoritative way that says that you belong in that space. Again, it's another way the brain works for, or against us. If something feels right then we tend to let it slide. We don't check, or at least we check less thoroughly.

An easy example of this to think of a building site. If you were to get on to the restricted area and you were wearing brand new trainers and a hoodie, how long do you think it would be before someone said, "Excuse me, what are you doing here?". Take the same example. This time you are wearing a high viz jacket, a hardhat, and holding a clip board, even if it's not the right clothes for that site and you don't have the same logo as everyone else. Chances are you might still raise suspicion but far fewer people would feel you felt out of place enough to stop and question you.

So, confidence is key. It shows you belong in that space. If you're a powerful person preparing to ring through and speak to another powerful person, then the receptionist is not likely to question you as much as if you perceive yourself as a low-level trainee that just got up from flipping burgers in Burger King. You convey your confidence though your tone, your language and even your posture and dress.

How can your dress or posture effect your confidence over the phone? Well, let's start with your posture. Did you ever see a live singer with a powerful voice sit down or slouch while they sing? No. never. It wouldn't happen. The reason for this is because your voice is more powerful when you stand, so if you are not going to stand (and I would recommend you do), you should at least sit upright. This also gives other people the impression you're not a slouch. As we covered in the survive part of the book, the same goes for your dress. If you remember, we covered this also. How you dress affects how you feel, and that affects how you sound.

You are going to need to be confident, sound authoritative and be direct.

That's what we mentioned earlier about having an air of authority around you like a judge or a police inspector would. When you ask for something, ask for it firmly, clearly and directly. Don't ask in a roundabout way.

Avoid things like "I-Is b-bbbill in today?" Ring through and say, "This is Stephen Joseph calling for Bill." In that example, we are not being rude. We are just conveying that we want to speak to Bill. We have told her who we are. We are not hiding it; however, the underlying tone says, "I'm important and busy. I told you what I need and I don't expect to be questioned."

Remember, as brutal as it sounds, receptionists are employed to be a facilitator of requests. All day long people ask to speak to people and they connect them. They are given tasks and they complete them. They do whatever and go wherever their leaders tell them. So, by their very nature they are used to being told what to do without questioning it. You just need to make her feel like you are one of the people she can't, or shouldn't, question, rather than one of the ones she can.

Sound familiar?

Another method you can use or combine with others is to sound familiar. We've said people don't tend to question what feels right. In the case above we were not questioned because she felt we were senior to her and that we knew Bill. In this technique we are going to use the same leverage, only this time from a familiar point of view.

If you know, for example, the receptionist's name (you may have gathered this information on a previous failed attempt that she would have forgotten by now), you can use this to your advantage. You can use his first name in a very casual way. So if you say, "Good morning. This is Stephen Joseph calling from xyz recruitment company. May I please speak with Mr. Senior Biller Executive, please?", that's going to be a very weak way of attempting the DM. You're instantly going to declare that you're a salesperson, and you're going to be instantly given the stops.

Using the familiar method, you might say something like, "Hi Sally. Is Bill around? It's Steve." And then, again in a very familiar way, you sound like you belong there. You know her name. You referred to him by his first name where other people in the business might not, confusing the gatekeeper, causing her not to question you. She will more likely pretend to know you, as you knew her, and be really polite to you.

You can take this one step further if you know anything about your prospect, e.g. if he likes golf or supports a football team.

This might work like this: -

> YOU: Hi Sally. Is Bill around? It's Steve.
> GK: No, he is offsite at the moment. What's the call regarding?

> YOU: On a lovely day today he is probably on the golf course! Thanks, Sally. Can you TELL him Steve called and I'll call him tomorrow.

End the call before she has a chance to question anything.

Or, alternatively;

> YOU: Hi, Sally. Is Bill around? It's Steve.
>
> GK: No, he is offsite at the moment. What's the call regarding?
>
> YOU: I'm not surprised after Chelsea's performance last night! No problem. I'll drop him a call tomorrow. Can you let him know Steve called, please?

End the call before she has a chance to question anything.

In both cases, you can see how we used information to gain credibility.

1. We know her name, and so we must either have spoken to her before or spoken to Bill about her.
2. We know Mr. Smith well enough to call him Bill.
3. We know about his hobbies or team.

You will also note that at no point did we answer her question and, finally, we TOLD her what to do, or what we will DO. There is no asking here.

This means that when we call back tomorrow, she will have to live up to the lie that she knows us as it would feel weird to question us.

Visualisations

The final thing I want you to consider in your mindset or approach to gaining your DM is visualisations. A visualisation is when you briefly take a moment, just a few seconds, to get your head right before you attempt each call, particularly the difficult ones.

Time and time again, I hear consultants saying things like, "I call her but she never picks up,", or, "I'll try, but there is no chance of me getting put through." Now, whether this is true or not is irrelevant. What is relevant is the negative state you are putting yourself in before you call. It's that defeatist attitude that *will* stop you from having any chance of reaching the DM.

So, before you dial the phone, I want you to pause and visualise the following things:

The prospect picking up the phone
The prospect being delighted you called
The prospect buying whatever it is you are selling
You closing the sale
You hanging up the phone
You feeling delighted after the call about what has just happened

This little inner story will only last a few seconds, but it will help your state as you dial through. As weird as it sounds and as ludicrous as it seems, it works, so you will just have to trust me on this one.

Chapter **17**

How to beat the gatekeeper: Methods, practice and examples

We have covered a number of states, tones, and misleading methods designed to confuse the receptionist and to make her question if she should stop you from being put through. To be honest, by practicing these and perfecting them, you will see a huge increase in your DM rate.

However, like I said, this is a big topic. We want to get all the DMs we can, and I want you to perfect this art, so I am now going to list my top methods for getting past the gatekeeper and gaining your DM.

Before we get stuck into to this topic, I want to highlight a simple fact, when we are trying to beat the gatekeeper, there are only two routes to the DM. These are where we go through the receptionist, or when we go around her. For the sake of simplicity, I have broken up the techniques here.

METHODS WHERE WE GO THROUGH RECEPTION

Method 1 – Show them love

Your first attempt should always be to just ask! After all, if we can secure the DM via the receptionist and build a relationship with her, then she will be able to help us with other connections in the future. So, it's worth putting in the time.

It's likely that this method is not going to impress you as you will already have been doing this and, presumably, not been getting far. So, if you have been trying this but getting little or no success, try empowering the receptionist to help you.

Example

> *"Julie, as much as I love our chats, I'm getting nowhere fast at the moment! I have been calling for John for ages now INSERT REASON WHY YOU NEED TO SPEAK TO THEM (For example, "I work with X client who is just like you. I need to speak to John as I want to show him how my candidates like Y can help him), but I just never reach him. Can you do me a favour and help me out? When will he be there or how can I reach him?"*

This is the simplest method, but you will be surprised how just asking will get you closer.

When to use:

First attempts or when you have called a lot and the receptionist knows you and likes you. Ideally, you will be in that friendly 'banter' stage with them.

Method 2 – Follow up email

Often, one of the stumbling blocks is when we get asked the pivotal question, "Does he know what this call's regarding?" Since we can't lie, this puts us in a tricky position. The easiest way to jump this is to email or post some information or literature prior to the call.

Now, the DM still won't be expecting your call, but this will give you enough to say yes to that question. After all, if you have sent him something it's only fair to assume that he would have read it and would be expecting your call. If you need more than that, it would be okay to say the call is, "in reference to the correspondence sent on May 5th." At least in that case it will make them feel as if they should be expecting your call, again putting pressure on them to just take the call rather than question it.

<u>Example</u>

> *"Does he know what the calls regarding?" "Yes, he does."*

or

> *"What's the call regarding?" "It's regarding the correspondence I sent last Thursday."*

 (avoid using vague language like, "Yeah, it's about the email I sent." It will lose the value.)

<u>When to use:</u>

This is another one to use early on. Once you have tried it a couple of times you're unlikely to be able to use it again since your cover is blown!

Method 3 – Control: Beat the receptionist by using selective words in a firm and authoritative tone

The trick here is to be evasive and give 'politician's answers'. Think, 'what do I currently say?' And ask yourself the question, 'do I need to say all of that?'.

If you can reduce the amount you give away about who you are and what you want, then the receptionist will have to keep asking you. She will eventually run out of patience and either be blunt with you or put you through.

The trick to not letting them get blunt with you is to use an authoritative tone to ensure you appear like a person of authority – after all the receptionist is not going to question a CEO, is she?

The second part to this method is to have "control" over the receptionist. This means that you are the one that asks the questions and she is the one that responds, and not the other way.

Look at the difference at the two examples below.

Receptionist: In Control

> **Consultant: Good Morning. Can I speak to Dave Smith, please?**
> *Receptionist: Who's calling?*
> **Consultant: It's Stephen Joseph from SJ Recruitment Services.**
> *Receptionist: I see..... She will now give you any of the following: -*
> *Dave is not in the office*
> *Dave is in a meeting*
> *Dave doesn't take sales calls*
> *Dave is out for the day*
> *Dave is not looking for agency help*
> *Dave is essentially doing anything other than wanting to speak to you!*

Now think, 'Who is in control here?' also, did we need to tell her so much so soon?

Try this example:

> **Consultant: Good Morning. This is Stephen calling for Dave Smith. Thank you.**
>
> Receptionist: What's the call regarding?
>
> **Consultant: Who am I speaking with?**
>
> Receptionist: His PA (did we ask her title?)
>
> **Consultant: What's your name?**
>
> Receptionist: Julie.
>
> **Consultant: Thank you, Julie. Can you TELL him that it's regarding the correspondence I personally sent him last Wednesday.**

Now, just reading this you can see how this is going to come across as very intimidating.

We haven't been rude, but she is going to feel the weight of this conversation. The key here is to say as few words as possible. Avoid the umms and errs; it will show weakness.

When we don't answer her question and in return, we ask her one, it immediately takes back control of the conversation (more on control later in the book).

You will also note that we TOLD her what to do and didn't ask.

Sometimes she will come back again with a further question. If this is the case, be ready with another thing to TELL her.

The general rule of thumb is you will get most on the first wave and the rest after three times of sending her back to the DM.

What happens is she will say to the DM, "Can you just take the call? This guy is a dick!" They will then puff their chest out and say something like, "Sure. Thanks, Julie. Put him through. I'll sort this guy out," and then you are through!

When to use:

After you have confirmed you are not going to get through with the direct-asking route, you should adopt this as your standard go-to. This method, once polished, will be the single most effective one here.

Method 4 – Voicemail

If the receptionist won't put you through, or if she is claiming that the DM is not at his desk, then ask the receptionist to put you through to a voicemail. They almost always will because it is deemed safe to do so.

Why should you do it?

1. The voicemail machine won't cut you off, so you can leave a full and detailed spec that the DM is likely to hear. If it's relevant, they will call back.

2. You can leave a vague message like, "It's Stephen. Can you give me call please on 07809,000,000?" They will have to call back as they need to know what it's about.

Note: This is a last resort as the DM is likely to be unhappy when they realise you are an agency and they have been tricked.

3. If they don't pick up, the standard message often lists the extension number which you can record and try at your own time.

Example

> *"You have reached extension number ONE ZERO FIVE. Please leave a message"*

When to use

Anytime you haven't tried it. This is one of your go-tos.

Method 5 – Referencing

The oldest trick in the recruiter's handbook – this one might be in your company's handbook it's that old. But like a lot of old things it has been forgotten, so dust this one off and give it a go. It's one of the easiest.

Simply find a reference to take and use this as a reason to beat the receptionist. If you are not calling about sales, then they will have to put you through.

When you call, make it explicitly clear that it is not a sales call. Don't let them have to guess.

> *"E.g. "Good Morning. This is Stephen Joseph calling for Dave Smith in connection with a reference for Jamie Miller. Thank you."*

SJ NOTE: -

1. You must take the reference properly when you get the DM. You can show expertise by saying something like, "Thank you for taking the call. I wanted to talk to you about Jamie. He came across really well, but he left mid-year, which always sets off alarm bells for me. I am considering him for a role over at x client. What're your thoughts?"

2. Depending on your sector, if you need the reference you may still have to send an online form. If this is the case, let them know on the phone to expect it.

3. Once you have taken the reference over the phone you can transition nicely by saying something like, "Thanks so much for that. It sounds like I have a winner. Listen, I wouldn't be doing my job if I didn't ask..." and away you go.

<u>When to use</u>

Anytime you get a reference to use. If you think you don't get this opportunity enough, simply jump on to CV Library or Reed and search for the company name. It will be easy to find people that worked at the same organisation that you can reference.

Method 6 – Nutmeg (still the most enjoyable one!)

In this one we are going to call the receptionist and dummy her with incorrect information in the hope the she corrects us (which they often do, and it's just wonderful).

It again plays on a psychological effect, and it gives them the power to make us feel stupid by correcting us which they will relish!

Example

It also works if you lead the receptionists with direct emails. This is great for businesses where getting direct emails can be more challenging as well. "If I can't speak to him, can I at least grab an email?" Then, "Is it first name dot last name @? Or...." Again, they will often feel the need to correct you if you have it wrong, or complete the sentence if you lead it.

When to use

Once your first round of friendly approaches has been exhausted.

Method 7 – Aim High

This one works if the DM you want to reach is a PA or someone who has a superior. If the DM is a PA and you ask to speak to him/her, you are likely to be screened by reception.

The trick here is to make it seem like you don't want the PA and you want the person above. If you approach the call that way, the receptionist will likely attempt protect the person above, and force you back to the PA who we really want.

E.g. if you want the CEO's PA, then call and ask for the CEO. The receptionist will then put you through to the person below him or her to "screen" you, which will likely be the PA.

The key is to ask for the CEO directly but this time be open about who you are, as we want to be 'caught out' on this one but we don't want them to suspect that you actually want the PA.

Method 8 - Play them off

Another method you can use is to play receptionists off each other. Often, you might have morning and afternoon receptionists. Naturally, one will be more favourable than the other. Get both of their names so you can use this information to your advantage.

One approach might be to call in the afternoon, say that you spoke with the morning receptionist and she said to call at 2.00 p.m. to speak to the DM. If you apply the right tone, you can make her feel like if she doesn't honour the request, it will make her look uninformed or disorganised. Another way we might use the name is to offer it up as information to make them feel like we belong there and it's safe to put you through.

In this example, I would call the afternoon receptionist by the morning receptionist's name in a really familiar way, as if to imply that we have been speaking a lot, then ask for the request.

Example

Consultant: Afternoon Julie. How's it going? Me again. I'm so sorry. I'm going to need Jeff again; can you pop me through?

Receptionist: This is Brenda. Julie left at 12.

Consultant: Of course. I'm so sorry, my love. It's Stephen. Jeff please...

If you do get stopped after this, it will only usually take one push back to get them as you have already established you belong there. So, if she hits you with a, "Sorry, Stephen, what's the call about?" you can just give a friendly but firm politician's answer, like, "No problem. Tell him it's Stephen Joseph. He will know."

Done. Through you go!

<u>When to use</u>

Anytime you have a reception desk with more than one person. Even if there is just one full-time receptionist, you will often find that there will be cover for lunch. So, do your homework and get the intel.

Method 9 - Risky, but be vague

The final method where we go through the receptionist is a last resort, as it is risky. If you are using this method, you will need to be prepared with a really strong call as you're likely to get in contact with the DM; however, they are likely to be pissed off when they realise you have tricked them.

All you need to do is to get the receptionist to pass on a vague message.

In this case you need to ring up the receptionist directly and then just ask for the DM directly (knowing full well she won't put us through). Say something vague like, "Is Bill there?" If she says, "No, what's it regarding?", say, "No problem. Can you just get him to return my call, please? It's Bill." Then leave your mobile number. They key here is to instruct her and rush her. You don't want her asking too many questions.

This one often works well because he's likely to call back (in the same way as the voicemail we discussed earlier). He has a message to call and he doesn't know who you are. This

117

means he has to call to make sure it isn't something important. Again, this is a risky strategy because when he calls back, he's likely to be pissed off.

So, as I have said, you will need to have a strong call planned and you will need to work fast to secure his interest. After this, your odds of getting him back on the phone are slim to none. So, make sure you secure a meeting or at least proper contact methods.

When to use

Absolute last resort. It's way too risky, but if you have tried everything and you are getting nowhere, then it's worth a shot.

METHODS WHERE WE GO AROUND RECEPTION

Method 10 – Timing

Look for patterns in the timing that you attempt to call and the patterns when it connects.

It's an obvious one, but so often we call at the same time every day, give or take 10-15 minutes, and never reach them. If that is the case, then make sure we call at a different time. Equally, if we have caught the DM 2-3 times in the past, look for a pattern in the timing when did we reach them.

It is for this reason that you must log all your calls, even your non-connected ones. Everything is data we can use to our advantage.

For example, if we have gained a direct dial but they never pick up the phone, then it's no use to us. The direct dial will help us avoid the receptionist, but it won't help us get him to pick up the phone, will it? So, we need to confirm every time we learn he is not at his desk, and, if we have caught him a few times in the past, when was he there.

Now, just because he picked up the phone at 10.04 a.m. on a Wednesday, that doesn't mean he will every Wednesday, but it will give you better odds. Most of us have a fairly structured day where lots of routine is applied.

Method 11 – Catching them napping

This one is a gem and they will never see it coming. Simply send some marketing or a bulk email when you know your client is not at work. Bank Holidays, Easter and the Christmas period are the best times for all businesses, but often certain sectors have their unique down days. "Why would I want to do this when you know no one is going to see it?", I hear you ask.

Simple. It's the bounce backs/out of office replies we want because the DM will often drop their guard in 'holiday mode' and not realise that we will see the message. A good proportion of the time the out of office replies will have their extension, other contact information, or even the sacred mobile number which we can record for the database. This will help us reach the DM in the future.

The 'Play Dumb' Methods

These methods play off the following three factors: -

1. Humans naturally want to help others.
2. The only person paid or briefed to stop you going through to the DM is the receptionist.
3. There is almost always an ext. number list next to every phone in every organisation.

I bet there is one on your desk now?

Method 12– It's not me, it's you

Most large organisations have a menu system when you call which welcomes you and gives you your options for each department, etc. In this example, rather than doing the norm and hitting zero or whatever for reception, you want to hit any other number. So, to be clear, I want you to intentionally go through to the wrong department. We want to speak to ANYONE who is not the receptionist.

Once you get anyone else to speak to you, you simply act surprised and ask them to either transfer you to the DM or give you the direct number.

Example.

> *"Hey John, it's Steve… Ohh, you're not John, are you?" "No, this is the kitchen, mate." "OMG, I am so sorry. Can you pop me through to John?"*

Last method – Random dial

This one uses the same technique as the last. We are trying to get anyone to pick up the phone and play out the same scenario, only this time you are going to do it by guessing the extension number.

When you call the number and the menu system kicks in and starts reading you your options, you can often just free type in a number and it will transfer you directly.

So, this one is long-winded as it involves a lot of trial and error but it does work.

> **SJ TIP:** *Most phone systems use a three-digit code and most start with 1 or 2. Try 105 or 210 to start you off. Then simply work your way up and down the extensions until someone picks up.*

This method is especially helpful when you are calling out of hours. The receptionist will put on the night service when they leave, and it will appear that you can't get through the menu system, but if you just dial the extension it will normally still transfer you.

How it works

I would guess a random code until you get any person to pick up.

When they do, go straight in and assume it's the DM.

> *"Oh, hi. Is this Bill?"*

When they say no, I'll say,

> *"My apologies. I had 230 written down as Bill's extension number. Is that not correct?"*

And then, because these people aren't trained to be protecting the DM, more often than not they will say,

> *"Oh, no. I don't know where you got that from. He's on 429."*

and you say,

> *"Ah, my apologies. Thank you very much,"*

and now you have his extension number. Now, it's just a matter of getting him at his desk.

Also, once you have one extension number and you have learned the format, it's much easier to work your way up and down the extensions to find other people in the organisation. This might seem a little laborious, and it is, but to get around the gatekeeper and get in front of your contact it's worth the time.

Productive calls

It doesn't matter one inch to me if you make five hundred calls to the receptionist (attempts, or non-DMs) today and the guy next to you made one call. If it was to a DM, he's far more likely to get a deal.

Remember, harsh though it is, you're in recruitment now. You get paid for results, not effort, so beat those gatekeepers and love the process, too. It's great fun.

Always get something

Have intention on every single call. This means two things: 1. that we are picking up the phone for a reason, and 2. that we will get something out of even a 'bad' call or a non-DM call.

Try to get something out of every call you make. As I said before about productive calls, there is only value if you achieve something. Ideally, you will reach your DM and make your pitch. However, if you're picking up the phone and you're making a call, even if you don't get the contact or it doesn't go the way that you have hoped, make sure you get something out of it.

For example, an easy way to make sure you've secured something on that call and have not wasted your time is to try to get a name or try to find out parts of the contact's routine. I.e., do they have Wednesdays off? Do they work in the mornings? If it's appropriate and you find out they have children, a wife, a dog, they support a particular football team, or something about the way that they work, then that's going to help in the way discussed previously.

If you only have a first name but don't have a last name, grab that. If you've got a general reception telephone number rather than a direct one, grab that. If you can get a direct number just by asking, then get that while you're there.

Principally, if you can do this, then at least you'll be going forward, even if you're not going forward at the rate that you hoped. This is still better than standing still or going backwards.

> *"Direction is better than speed. Many people are going nowhere fast."*

Chapter **18**

Gatekeeper summary

So, now you are armed and ready to do battle with the gatekeepers across the land. You now have my top techniques, routes and tones to use to beat the gatekeeper. These are just the ones that I know and have used for years. You may be able to combine some and you may come up with your own, but one thing is for sure.

For the first attempt, just call through and ask in a friendly tone.

If she doesn't connect you, it's at that moment the game begins. You MUST be asking yourself, is the DM just not there, or is she screening my call? For example, if she says he isn't in the office, then he might actually just be out of the office. If this is the case, you simply need to call back when he is. She might not be stopping you from going through.

BUT: if you feel the gatekeeper is hindering you from reaching the DM, then you know that you can't ask her directly ever again as you will be simply wasting your time.

So, from then on out, record the method you tried, take notes on people's names and remember their voices. Gather data, what they do, when they do it etc. Map it out so you can start to predict movements.

Then, have a clear and focused intention to get them on the phone – everything starts with intention.

And, most of all never, ever, ever give up! The receptionist needs to know that you are not going away. Often you can just wear them down.

Remember, though this is a difficult task, it's like riding a bike. You have to practise. You can't just give it a try and, if it doesn't work, go back to sending an email and crossing your fingers. You now have the information. Use it, keep it, and practise it. Once you become proficient you really will be able to get most people on the phone after a short period which WILL make your career thrive.

Beating the gatekeeper is a wildly documented topic. This means you can learn more. So, study it, read books, get on YouTube, and get on the audiobooks. Find out as much as you can about this specific topic, because the more you know about getting the DM on the phone and beating the gatekeeper, the more calls you'll make that are productive. Remember, it's productive calls that matter.

Real world applications of beating the gatekeeper

These skills have massive advantages both in work and out. Imagine if you wanted to get into banking, but the job requires a 1st from a Russell Group University and you have a 2:2 from London Met. Still, you think you could really excel for them.

What's going to happen if you reply to the advert and you get screened by HR? Nothing. Zero chance. You will be dead in the water. However, what if you flipped that and you took the time to find the CEO of Morgan Stanley or Wells Fargo, beat the gatekeeper and got him on the phone? Are you guaranteed a job? No, but you are going to at least get heard and have a shot, and even if you fail, you will undoubtedly impress him.

Same goes if you are a music artist or budding rapper and you want to get discovered. Sure, you could make a Soundcloud, or give out CDs, etc. But how many people are doing that? What're the odds of getting discovered in this day and age? Not a lot. Flip that again and imagine you got the CEOs of the top 20 record labels and played your music on the phone to them? If it was any good, then you would at least move forward much quicker.

Or, finally, what if you experienced bad customer service and the complaints team were not taking you seriously. What can you do? Not a lot. Flip that and image if you got the CEO of Vodafone on the phone and you told him about your customer experience. Do you think he would care? And if needed, could he put it right? No doubt.

So, as you can see, this is a very powerful skillset that has many uses. More so, it's a dying art. With cold calling on the decline, these skills are not getting practised and passed on. People are starting to say things like cold calling is dead and it doesn't work. Well, I'm here to tell you that's bullshit. Cold calling is alive. The only thing that's dead is people's ability to do it.

So perfect these methods, learn them, develop them, add your own and pass the skills on. Let's keep the trade alive!

Chapter **19**

Plan for and expect the no

Every time you pick up the phone to make a sales call, you need to plan for and expect the no. Now, I'm not saying we need to be pessimistic; I'm just saying it's highly likely, just by the nature of recruitment sales, that you're going to get a no more often than a yes in your opening calls.

So, don't be scared of the nos. Invite and expect them.

You know, it's likely that a lot of your calls will contain similar content. This means you are able to predict how it's likely to go. For example, you know when you say "X", they normally say "Y". If you can predict this with reasonable success, then you need to have a suitable response for that Y which will form part of your repertoire. So, start to plan the call out in your mind before you make it. This doesn't mean you plan to the nth degree so much so that you spend all day planning and no time calling (as we have discussed). It just means you need to expect the expected and do something about it.

The analogy I usually use with trainees is to try and think of your calls as a flow chart, i.e. you start at a certain pathway and then, depending on the response of the person, go left or right until you work towards the direction you want, each time anticipating and expecting the possible outcomes.

The reason you want to do this is so that you can start to sound confident in what you are saying. As we have learned, it's mostly about *how you* sound rather than exactly what you say, so by planning your words it will help you to deliver them well.

Now, this isn't something you can do in your first week as you need to collect some 'data' by making the calls. You need to know what works, what doesn't, where you lose them, and where you gain them. However, try to do this as soon as you can, as it's going to help you make more productive calls.

Chapter **20**

Park and recap

Once you have created a mental or physical flow chart for your calls and you are comfortable planning for and expecting the normal 'no's, you will find more calls get to their desired goal. Bingo! Once this happens you will need to park the call, since there is only so long you can keep a prospect on the phone. Your task should be to get as far as is sensible on each call, and then attempt to park the call in preparation for the next one where you will recap.

How to park

What I do in that scenario is summarise what's happened on that call, i.e. what's been agreed to, the contact method, contact frequency or any expected actions, at the end of each call. Then you book in the next call. Now, ideally this will be a specific date and time if that's sensible or possible; however, if it's not, you should loosely agree to a time that is most convenient for them.

This will help you for two reasons. One, it's going to be much easier to get through the gatekeeper and back to them if you have a solid first call under your belt. Two, you are going to be much better received on the second call if you have built some rapport the first time around.

How often you should call depends on your industry, your company's values and objectives, and the size and level of work the client has. However, as a rule of thumb it should be as often and as frequent as is sensible for you to stay in the mind frame of your contact.

How to recap

When you come back to the call that you've parked, you want to briefly open, remind the contact who you are and when you spoke last, and then briefly summarise where you got to and what you agreed to before continuing with today's call objective.

So, I would start by saying:

> ""Hi Jean. It's Steve over at xyz company. We spoke last week on Thursday regarding potential future vacancies and you mentioned there might be a recruitment strategy coming up once the budget becomes available at the end of the month. We agreed to speak today. Are you good to speak now?"

Now the prospect is not likely to remember the whole conversation so you can't expect the world, but what you are going to do is gain credibility and validity, and, crucially, not have to start from the beginning every time. *This* is how you progress a relationship!

She's going to remember, "Ah, I did have that conversation and I did make those commitments," and in that, you instantly gain a bit more rapport than if you'd started from the beginning. That puts you at a higher place with every conversation.

This method was designed for a fast-paced temp agency that you know the client is using every day or very frequently. In this scenario you should need no more than about three calls to be able to win a contact on board, as long as you've learned something, you've recapped, and you've progressed with each call.

By the time you've reached the third call you should be comfortably within the zone of being able to ask for and commit to some level of tentative buying.

So, now you know how to park and recap. This moves us nicely over to the next major factor as to whether you're likely to be successful on the phone. That is control.

Chapter **21**

Control

In this chapter of the book we're going to speak about control; being in control and having control of the conversation. So, by this point in the book we have covered a lot, such as getting the right person on the phone, having intention on the call, the way we want to position ourselves, and the way we want to think about the call. The final element is to understand what control is, what in and out of control looks like, and some suggestions on how to have control.

If you're already in recruitment but have not been that successful, in that you're regularly getting vacancies and you're regularly shortlisting what seem to be appropriate candidates but you're still not getting the deal over the line. This could be because you're not getting the interviews you need and you're not getting the client buy-in. The clients go cold and your contact dwindles along with your chances!

The truth is, this often has nothing to do with your candidates. In fact, more often than not it's more to do with your level of control. You may have even found that the candidate that ended up working for your client via a different agency was the same one you shortlisted, or maybe the candidate that eventually secured the role was of a lesser quality or less experienced than the one that you would have put in. This often baffles a lot of trainee recruiters. Again, the reason for this is often control.

So, if this sounds all too familiar, or if you're just starting out and want to avoid those traps, get to understand what control is, what it looks like, what it doesn't look like and how to have it.

What is control?

When we're talking about control, we're talking who is in the position of authority and who holds the power within the conversation. When you are in a conversation and you are under fire, answering all the questions and making all the responses, you are generally at the mercy of the clients every want and need. You are not in control.

A good example is to think of a constable interviewing a suspect. That's a very one-sided conversation.

The way that you gain control initially is to position yourself as a person speaking to another person on the same level. You don't need to be above or below them, although you will usually start below them in terms of control when you open a new sales call. Assuming your open was of interest to them, you should be able to settle the call down enough that you are speaking to them at the same level. This usually happens when they have subconsciously agreed that you have something of value to them or they he either chosen to, or are considering working with you. Now they're committed. They need something that you have.

If you have something that they want, then you will probably be sharing control and the conversation will be flowing nicely. It will 'feel' like a good call, and so you will probably expect good outcomes from it.

However, the process often goes astray when commitments are not made or the agreements and actions are not clearly understood, and that's often where people lose the control of the sale.

To use an example, imagine a call that the consultant typically might feel went well because they have been given a vacancy to work on by a client and they intend to send some good CVs. All good so far, but if there wasn't enough control exercised on the call, the client doesn't yet know how much they can rely on that particular agent, when to expect the CVs, or how long the turnaround will be. Therefore, this is where the sale often drifts off.

What happens all too often is by the time agent comes back to them with a sensible CV (which is often too long if you are a junior or trainee consultant), you've no idea of the status of that role. It could have been filled internally or they could have found a better applicant. Put simply, you just don't know what's going on with the client and his role, and this is because they didn't know what was going on with you!

An easy and efficient way to make sure you're always in control is to summarise the call at the end of it and agree on expectations and timeframes (similar to the park and recap we discussed earlier).

A simple call might go like this:

"Okay, great. I'll get a couple of CVs over to you for that specific role. I should have completed my initial shortlisting by midweek and, by the time I've qualified the remaining candidates, I'll have a couple over to you by the end of the week. I'll probably send them Thursday evening with the intention of catching up Friday afternoon to get your thoughts. If you could double-check in the meantime on the duration of the role, this would help. Does that sound okay with you?"

In this example, the client knows the timeframes involved and he knows what you're going to do. This adds validity (which helps to show the value in your fee) and, more importantly, they know not to do anything else about filling this role since there is an action and an agreed timeframe to go back on. Essentially, they will put down the phone feeling much more confident that their needs are being met, which should be your aim.

Also, by suggesting the timeframe, you offer the client a chance to agree with it or suggest a new one if that doesn't work for them. Again, as always, it's about working towards the deadlines of the client, not you.

Effort in: Reward out

Another way that you can influence control is to regularly make it easy for a yes by addressing the effort in, reward out ratio. I.e., you're going to do lots of work on this for them, and all they need to do is say yes. That's a very low effort in, high reward out equation.

An example of this might be, "Okay, so, as we are on a deadline on this, I'm going to stay late tonight to make sure that the adverts go out today. I'm going to write detailed bespoke adverts and I'm going to place them on the top five main job boards. I'll have to speak to my boss, but we can probably get premium credits for this, too. They will need two or three days to circulate, on average. After that, I'm going to go through the initial screening process over the phone. I'll then invite in the best three candidates for a face to face meeting at my office and screen them through until I've found the best suitable applicant.

I should have all that done by Thursday, so either way I'll give you a call on Friday morning to briefly give you an overview of the candidate that I've selected on your behalf. Assuming you're happy, you just give me a quick yes and they can start on Monday. Does that sound okay with you?"

It's probably the most exaggerated example I could have given, but you can see how you much control you're going to have by using the summary and the effort in, reward out ratio. Remind them they need to put minimal effort in to get maximum opportunity out, and you can get a lot of good results by positioning your calls in that way.

Forward, remind, recap

Another method I use to have control is to recap everything that we discussed via email at the top of an old email they haven't responded to. Now, I don't mean to create "War and Peace", but when you put down the phone, if they haven't looked at your CVs for example and they said they would, I would simply take the CVs you sent the first time out of your outbox and forward them. Leave the time and date stamp at the top and then put few lines at the top recapping the last call with the old message below, "Thanks for agreeing to look at these again. As promised the CVs are attached. I'll catch up with you on Friday to see what your thoughts are." And each time you have any communication with regards to following up on those CVs, I would resend it.

Now, this may seem like overkill for you and it may seem unnecessary, but you've got to remember that hiring managers are very busy people. The recruitment element in their role is usually only a very small part of what they do, and they're likely to have lots of agents with lots of candidates and lots of emails. So, in the spirit of the effort in, reward out ratio, make it easy for them! Rather than them having to search through their inbox, find where they saved it or admit to you that they've ignored your email because they actually had no intentions of reading it, it appears magically in their inbox, just a few seconds after the call with that reassuring Microsoft "Bing!".

Make it easy for your CVs, your agency, your telephone number to be found. This way it's always an easy route for them to come back to you. You'll be surprised how often by just adding this to your routine will increase your sales – it's busy out there and its competitive! Give yourself the edge and the chance to be seen!

To summarise:

To gain control over conversations ensure that, once you have settled the call and you are on the same level, you take control by summarising the call, highlighting the actions and setting the precedent for the next call. You should also leverage the effort in, reward out ratio as often as possible and always forward any email communication that's necessary with every call, especially if it's CVs! Countless roles are lost not because the CV was no good, but because the CV was never looked at!

On that note, if you are shortlisting more than one vacancy, then always break them up in to two emails with clear titles. The reason, again, is because they will often get forwarded on to different managers and you don't want them to break your email up. That would be too much work (with a poor effort in, reward out ratio) and it might not happen. Tip the balance, change the ratio and separate the emails.

"What you lack in skill, make up for in numbers"

This is a famous quote by Jim Rohn, one of the influential speakers I often reflect on and quote. This quote is a great adage for the way to think about sales while you are refining your craft in the twelve months.

It goes back to what I said at the start; you need to be overdelivering everything you can in the first six months. This should form your expectations and *your* standard. You need to always, always exceed your minimums. As a reminder, minimums are just that. They are minimums. If you shoot for a minimum and you fall short, then now you are underperforming and that's not a place you want to be in your first six months; so, always increase your own personal standard and overdeliver whatever minimums you are given.

If you are sitting next to a top biller, you will notice he is probably going to make a lot less outbound calls than you. He might not even make any. He might only be getting inbound calls and inbound clients. And yet he will be easily able to generate massive sums of business with fairly minimal output.

Because of this, it would be easy for you to get the impression that it's going to be easy to for you to do the same and achieve the results he has. Hopefully, you know by now you can't do this! What you don't see is all the work he's done previously, prior to you joining, that gained him those clients. That is exactly the same as the work you are being asked to do now. If you want to gain his knowledge and respect, show the man the respect he's due. Sit yourself next to him and double any output he does. This is simple: -

Output input maths

If you can double the outputs he does and you are half as good, then you are getting close to matching the pipeline and the forthcoming results that he will experience.

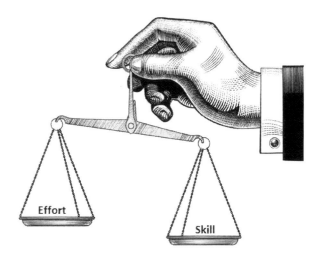

Apply this thinking to everything you touch. Make it another way to set up your stall in your mind about the way in which you go about attacking the first twelve months of your recruitment career. If you can do this long enough and consistently enough, you'll soon be on the other side of the fence. You'll be a top producer having someone sit next to you, looking to match your work.

Always be the hardest working man in the room.

A lost pound

I recently came about this story when I was reading an article by Grant Cardone, I think, and it's actually really referenceable to what we do and our work. I started quoting it in my material in training new consultants, and it was very effective. This simple story has a hidden message which is really applicable to our role.

If you look around any medium- or large-sized recruitment business, you're going to see some real winners and you're going to see some people that are really struggling. Trainee consultants tend to get the most stressed or the angriest during their first twelve months because they have a lot of pressure to deliver and they've got so much riding on so few deals.

Most of the time when a deal goes bad, it's because of something you did or didn't do. Perhaps you didn't exercise as much control over something as you could have. Naturally, you get upset, maybe even irate, as that might have been the deal you needed to make to get yourself out of performance management, into the commission bracket you wanted, or, even worse, to pass probation. The point I am making here is that one or two deals are going to be infinitely more important to you than they will be to the top performers in the room. I am sure by now you are thinking, "Yeah, I get that Steve. That's obvious, what's your point here?" Well, let me tell you the story.

Story time

The story goes there are two brothers and they're both given a pound by their father to go and buy chocolate as a treat. Happy in their new found fortune and eager to get their chocolate, they both hurry to the local store. They're understandably excited and are both having fun and skipping and running along when tragedy hits (I added the drama!). One of the brothers trips and falls down, grazing his knee. Worse still, his pound falls out of his hand and rolls down a nearby drain, gone forever. I am sure you can see where the story is going. The other brother obviously held his pound tightly and managed to have his chocolate bar. His day ended in joy, whereas the clumsy brother who lost his pound was obviously upset and returned back home with no chocolate and no pound.

When he returns home, he goes to see his father to explain what happened. This is when the father delivers the lesson. "Son," he says, "the problem wasn't that you lost the pound. The problem was that it was your only pound."

Now, I'm not sure why the brother couldn't have shared his chocolate, or the father couldn't have given him a second pound. I guess if either of those things had happened, it wouldn't have made for such a strong fable. However, I liked that story and thought it was powerful. What you take from that will vary. It could be about excess, greed, supply and demand, or just a tight father and a mean brother.

What made it relatable for me was that it is the same as the trainee consultant I described at the beginning of this chapter pinning all his hopes on that one deal. Stop and think; if you are so devastated about one particular deal that didn't go through, it's probably not because *that* deal is so important. It's more likely because of your lack of pipeline. If you had five or six deals in the process or another equally valued deal, you would be far less bothered if one big or a couple of smaller deals didn't go through.

What's the moral of my story? Never put too much energy into one deal. After all, the outcome, as always, is at best 50/50. Hedge your bets and always make sure to include some new business development time (this will help you avoid the yo-yo effect we discuss later). Of course, we want every deal to go through, and sometimes you get lucky and back-to-back deals go in, but you also get losing streaks as where back-to-back deals don't go in. What's important is that you always maintain your pipeline, which, if done correctly, will protect you from the ups and downs.

One final note on pipeline. Avoid focusing too much on one part of the pipeline. Too much client work but not enough candidate work, too much interviewing but not enough advertising, too much marketing but not enough business development still puts you in the same dangerous position. You need to make sure, at least in the three-sixty model, that you are ticking all of the boxes regularly so that you don't end up focusing on one pound or one role. Otherwise you, like the boy, might end up hungry and embarrassed with a grazed knee.

Chapter **22**

Speed and efficiency

Speed and efficiency are now your best friends. If you haven't already gathered, you're going to be working lots of hours, but there are a maximum number of hours you can work. Once you get to that level, the next thing that comes in to play is how much can you get done within those hours. That's where speed and efficiency come in.

Look at two people within the office working exactly the same number of hours. However, one is delivering twice the output (or more likely five times) as the other in an even playing field. How can that be? Sure, it's partly skill, but the second part is efficiency.

Speed and efficiency are your next big hack to beating the game. There are a number of ways you can help yourself in this area, the first of which is to standardise your administration tasks.

Recruitment tends to have a high degree of administration. It's important, but not revenue making. Therefore you want it out of the way in the quickest and most efficient way, and, as always, I have a few tips you might not be using.

Email templates

You'll find quickly, after being in the business for two or three months, that you are often writing the same or very similar emails to candidates or clients. It might be to confirm an interview, an appointment or to send information about a job spec etc. The variations will be wide. However, what I guarantee you will find is, if you look at your outbox at the end of the week, more than 60% of the new emails (not replies or chains) can be grouped in to about five to fifteen emails that you send all the time (or variations of them).

It still to this day amazes me that I see countless businesses typing those emails every time from fresh. It's time consuming, creates errors, and often doesn't get done because of other pressures. This causes you problems further down the line. My solution: just make a template! Now some businesses have caught this trend and they will have them in place, but in my experience a surprising amount still don't. If that's you, then listen up!

Now, it's not important that your template is word for word perfect and exactly the same every time. I personally don't like templates to be used in that way. However, it should have 80% of the message ready for you to just top and tail the email with a few lines to make it more specific to that conversation.

I'd soften a template and make it less template-like with a few lines like:

"Great to speak to you today, Jenny. I can't believe that you have family from the south coast, too. It's such a small world! I'm looking forward to catching up more when we meet next week. Please find confirmation below, as discussed."

Aside from the speed and efficiency hack with templates, they are also a good way to gain consistency in the business as well.

How do you create a template?

Well, it depends on what system you use and what you have available. However, one system we all use daily is Microsoft Outlook. It's the most common email application and there is a way to do it in this system. Now, our own software has the ability to add templates; however, I still use the Outlook system as the templates are right there where I need them, when I need them.

What you need to do is create a signature (a signature is the standard text and image set up that appears at the bottom of every email you type automatically). Now, you will already have a signature applied which will be your default. When you click 'new email', the system will automatically load your standard signature, which is usually your name, job title, contact number, and company logo.

You can use the same tool to create countless signatures, which we will use as templates. Then, once you open your email and you need to send a template, you will simply open your email, click signatures, and it will give you a drop down of all the signatures or templates that you have made.

How to create a signature template.

Open a new message.

Click on the message tab.

Click on 'Signature'

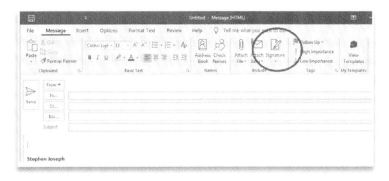

Go to the bottom of your available signatures and click Signatures...

That will then open the Signatures and Stationary box.

Click New

And then name your 'template'.

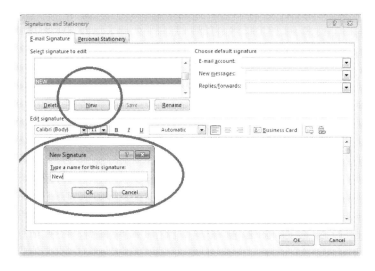

In this example we have called it 'new'

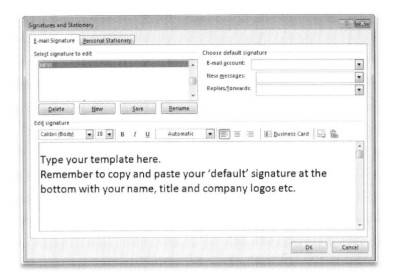

You can then free type your template in the box at the bottom and click OK.

TASK

Have a look at last week's outbox and work out what the top 10 emails you send are. Once you have them, take some time over the weekend to really polish them and make sure they are grammar perfect, slick, and really deliver your message and brand. Once you have them, save them as a template and name them something appropriate like 'Meeting Confirmation'.

I'm sure by now you can see how this is going to help with speed and efficiency but think for one second about how it also impacts on your business development. Imagine how impressed the client is going to be when you put down the phone and 30 seconds later a confirmation email comes into their inbox! What message does that send? It shouts these guys are on it, they are organised and they are professional, and that consultant does what he says.

Take that versus what happens at present. You promise you will send the email and, because you are busy and want to focus on the things that directly generate revenue, you either quickly send a sloppy email with grammar errors or a good strong email but at 8.00 p.m. two days later. I'm sure you can guess which is the most effective and which creates the type of 'image' you want to portray.

Email templates will help you to show a level of expertise, a level of reliability, and a level of credibility. It shows that you're going to do what you said. Overall, you're going to score high in the client's mind. You're going to send them the information you said you would, which often gets overlooked. Finally, you're going to be able to send a clear and concise message as effectively as you can because you've written it a million times before.

Use email templates/signatures to help you with speed and efficiency and getting free of the admin side of the role.

Read receipts, delivery receipts, and gaining time!

Another useful tool available in Outlook which will help you with speed and efficiency is delayed emails, delivery receipts and read receipts. So, I'll cover them next.

Read receipts and delivery receipts

So, to start with we'll discuss read receipts and delivery receipts; if you're not familiar with these tools, they are exactly what they say (god bless Microsoft for keeping it simple!). A delivery receipt is an email receipt sent from the server of the person you are emailing to your server; it's automated and it simply says the email you sent got there. This is useful when you are sending an email for the first time, if you have guessed the email address, or if it's an email with a large attachment that might have been delayed or stopped due to its size. You will want to use this tool to confirm that the message you sent reached its intended place.

A read receipt is an email receipt that gets sent to you when the person you sent an email to reads it. This is a very handy tool. However, you should know that it is optional for the reader of the email to send a receipt, so it's not 100% reliable. It's possible for you to ask for a read receipt and the recipient can still read the email without sending a receipt back. So, like all of these tools, use them but don't rely on any one solely. Again, there is a degree of ethics around this. Some people consider it rude, so, again, check with your company about their stance on this. However, I personally feel it is appropriate, and I use them often.

If you are given free rein to use them, I would suggest you do, and the reason is this; it acts as an information tool and information is power in our game. If you send an email which, for example, has a shortlist with some suitable CVs and you're wondering when the natural time to follow up that email is, well, the best time to do that is as soon as you can after your client has seen the CVs, if not before.

If they opened your email and it's been a while since you sent it, you'll get a read receipt there and then. Well, good news my friend. They are probably sat at their desk looking at your CVs. So, now would be a great time to ring and talk them through with the DM. This also helps you to beat the gatekeeper because if they claim they're not in the office, it's very easy for you to confirm that you know they're in the office since they just opened the email you sent. They are more likely to take your call as you are discussing that particular email.

You can use the read receipt to find out a) the email has been read and b) when it was read. It forms part of your package to know more about their movements in general, i.e. when they're usually at their desk, when they are looking at those particular pieces of information, and of course, when you can follow up, with the ideal time being right now!

How to create a 'Delivery Receipt' or a 'Read Receipt'.

Open a new message.

Click on the Options tab

Select either or both, Delivery Receipt, or Read Receipt.

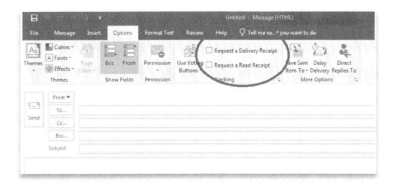

How to gain time

Whilst you're there in the email, Outlook offers a wonderful tool called delayed email. It's a hugely useful tool that people don't seem to use or know about but will help you massively with speed and efficiency.

It does just this. If you type an email now, but you would like it to go out at midnight, then you can simply delay the email time. Once you have done this, it will sit patiently in your Outlook outbox until the time passes. Then it automatically sends the email.

There are a couple of really useful applications for this. For example, if you want to send it to a different country that's in a different time zone or if you're in a large country that has different time zones, then you can send it so it arrives at the appropriate time in the inbox you are sending it to. Again, this will give it the maximum chance of being read. For example, if it is sent during the business day, it might be midnight on the other side of the world. That's not a particularly useful time if you're dealing with someone that gets a lot of emails and information coming to them. It is possible and likely that your email will get lost or at the very least looked at much later.

However, if you delay the email so it arrives at 9.30 a.m. or 9.00 a.m. when they're sat down at their desk, again, the chances of your email being read are much, much higher. So, you can delay your email for that purpose.

Another sneaky reason you might want to apply it is if you want to give the impression to your client that you've been working on a vacancy into the small hours. Maybe you promised the client that you're going to stay late so you can show commitment, but you found what you needed much quicker than expected. Again, you can simply send the email to the client at about 5.30 p.m. and delay it to 8.46 p.m. so that the client thinks you've been working all the way through the night, you've left work late just so you could deliver on what you promised, thus gaining credibility in their mind. When they see that it's arrived at that particular time it has an impact (as long as you follow up!); however, what actually happened is that you got the job done and you got off to the pub and had a quick pint rather than working late. Everybody is a winner! You, the client, and the landlord!

One the flip side, you might want to make sure your information is the first email in their inbox each day. If your client starts early, at 7.00 a.m. for example, and you don't get in until 8.30 a.m., you can delay an email until 7.10 a.m. As most people grab a coffee and check their emails first, your email will arrive just as the DM is checking, again increasing your odds of it being read. We use this a lot in my office as always want to be first with the information early in the day. Now we are in early anyway however we are busy so we use to this to buy time, by prepping quality information the night before.

How to delay an email

Open a new message

Click on the options tab

Select 'Delay Delivery'

Under the 'Delivery Options' section you can click 'Do not deliver before'.

And then choose your date and time.

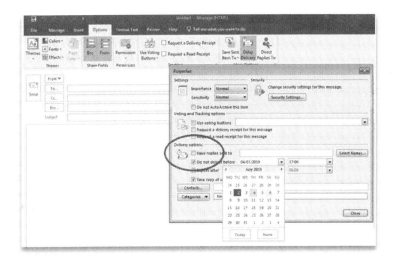

As you can see, delayed emails and read receipts are really powerful tools in making sure you get your information to the right people at the right time and making sure you maximise speed and efficiency - which, combined with using templates, will increase the chances of your communication being seen.

TASK

Write down three ways that you might use a delayed email and three ways you might use a read receipt.

Chapter **23**

Communication

In our next chapter, we're going to talk about communication and how it's changing.

There's a lot of debate in the recruitment world about the future of recruitment, the way we communicate, and how the way roles are filled is changing. Whether you think the future is bleak or prosperous, one thing is for sure - it is changing.

How much that applies to us right now, I'm not sure. One thing is for sure the way; the way we communicate is definitely moving forward. Now, I personally don't believe that anytime in the near future there will be a more effective method than picking up the phone and speaking. However, I have had to recently reevaluate my thoughts on this, so it's definitely a topic worth looking at. I'll share my thoughts with you.

If you think about how you communicate with your friends or in your social groups these days, it's very rarely over the phone, in fact a recent study suggests that ¼ of all smartphone users, never make a call! So long gone are the days of your teenage daughter blocking the line as she chats to her friend for hours on the landline. In fact, very few of us even have a landline at home anymore.

A study by Ofcom ,the UK communications watchdog, reports that between 2012 and 2017 minutes of landline calls fell by 52%.

More often than not these days, your personal communication might come via text message, email, WhatsApp (a very popular communication tool especially for groups), or you might even be using instant messaging via Facebook or Instagram.

If you think about the methods in which you communicate with your friends in your social groups, it isn't going to be so different when we come to work with our business contacts and our business candidates. Now, there is some debate about the social barrier here and you need to avoid from crossing the line. After all, we are in uncharted territory with this stuff as the lines about what is work communication and home communication are blurry ones at best. You need to do what is appropriate for you, your company, and your sector.

In our job, which is principally about communication, it's useful at least to be aware of the different methods that you can use to keep a good line of communication open. Be aware your company is likely to have an ethical standpoint on this or they're likely to have an opinion over what's appropriate and what's not. My advice is to check before embarking on any of these routes.

If you're given free rein, you should be aware there is more than just the phone as a method of communication now, although I can't stress enough that should always be the default.

Pros and cons

Email is very embedded in everything thing we do now and is far from a new tool. We are almost always requested to follow up every call with a confirmation email. You can still use it for prospecting candidates or to try and gain interest, but remember two things. It is only useful <u>if</u> it is read, and make sure you monitor your tone. It's very easy to upset someone with a poorly worded email which is another reason why I like to use templates. So, use it carefully and only ever as a supplement to your calls. Never use it as your primary method as prospecting. Every week I receive about 5-10 emails from companies who are trying to sell me things or services via email. Often, they are not even products I want and as I obviously don't reply, they just email again and again, it's just not going to work.

WhatsApp is a great tool. It's pretty widely accepted now to be a safe method of communication and it's not abnormal to WhatsApp someone you don't know. The pros are that groups are easy to form, so it's especially handy to communicate a message with a large group of people, and you can see if the message has been delivered and read, so there is a degree of checking. The cons are that it can be difficult to get your full message across as your text message space is limited and, like email, your tone can be read wrong, so it's best used to confirm something or to drive a call to action.

Its also worth noting that if you are going to use WhatsApp, remember to have a suitable photo, if you're using your personal account and you have a picture of you and the boys, shirts off in Napa, however good the trip was, it might not send the image you're looking for.

LinkedIn, if your sector uses LinkedIn, it can be a great tool. Often called the business Facebook, it's widely accepted that you can message people you don't know here. Again, make sure you use it as a supplementary tool. Because it's so widely accepted you can message people, it's also accepted that it's not rude to ignore the message. It's become like spam email and junk mail. Content gets often overlooked.

SJ TIP: *If you are using it to drive sales, make sure your message is strong, clear, relevant and about your prospect, not you. I see so many messages that are about what the company does, has achieved, or what its goals are, etc. Whilst there might be a need to contain some of these elements, you need to make sure that the message focuses around what you can do for the prospect or how you can help with their goals and targets.*

Instagram and Facebook messaging, for the most part are still personal communication tools, and I think it's fair to say it would still seem weird to get a business message through those channels. So, for me they are still just outside of the norm. That said, our job is to communicate and as long as the way you go about it is correct, they can be useful and very effective. If it helps you get your candidate or DM, then go for it. Just remember if you are using these methods, you are getting into people's personal lives. So, you should ensure your communication is professional, avoid getting too casual or flirty, make sure that your profile and pictures are appropriate, or ideally use a business account.

If you are planning to use social media messaging it's easy to build a database or online presence through #tags, check ins, likes and shares etc., these can all be driven by fairly cheap but effective competitions or giveaways. Obviously we need to be sensitive to GPDR these days but assuming you have the all clear from the legal team you could run a competition for a new Macbook Air for example, and all candidates need to do is visit the office, check in, and post a picture of them using your #tag and tag one friend. You run the competition for a month and then a candidate is drawn at random. If it's promoted effectively you can see how wide your message, brand or offer could go in front of a targeted audience, very powerful.

Landline. Yeah, remember that? Surprisingly, we have moved so far away from our landlines these days that people have stopped calling them, chalking them up as being too personal. Well, that's just perception and not reality, so if you have a landline number, especially for a candidate, you should absolutely call it. Let me tell you this; these days when the landline rings in our house, we pick it up. The reason is that it doesn't ring much, and it gives that feeling of, "I better pick it up as I don't know what it's about." The opposite is applicable for my mobile. If I don't know the number, it's going to voicemail.

If you have a landline number, you should ring it and you should even take the time and effort to try and capture them for your database, when you're on a call to a candidate if it's not listed on the CV, ask 'what's your landline number?'. You see, the more options and methods we have to communicate, the better. Just remember you need to call at a time that is suitable. If you call a landline to reach a candidate at home at 11.00 a.m., they are likely going to be at work. So, always call 6.30 a.m. before they leave for work or post 6.30 or 7.00 p.m. once they are home.

Twice-dialled I was also trained to always dial twice every time we ring. Again, you will be surprised how often this simple trick works simply because people often ignore the first call. The reason they will often pick up on the second goes back to that perception thing. They think that if they are ringing twice, it might be important, so I better pick it up.

When it comes to communication methods, make sure that you're looking at, reviewing, and gathering different methods of communication with your candidates and your clients so you can be in their minds and you can reach them when you need to get them. This allows you to effectively communicate your message.

When it suits them, not us

My final rule, and the art of communication with clients and candidates, relates to timing. It has to be when it suits the candidate or the client, not you. Remember, if they're at work all day and you can't speak to them, well, that means you're going to need to make some calls in the evening.

Time and time again I'm told the candidates lapsed and we can't get a hold of them, when actually we've called them every day at 11.00 a.m. for the last week. Well, at 11.00 a.m. they're probably at work, so as we have discussed they're not likely to pick up the phone.

You need to use contact times and contact methods to suit your candidates and your clients.

If you take a bunch of CVs home with you of candidates you can't reach and ring the landline twice after 9.00 p.m., I guarantee you will get a much higher response rate. Try it. The response you get will be amazing.

Chapter **24**

Continue to develop yourself

Hiring managers for trainee recruiters often like to see someone with entrepreneurial flair. Just having a good degree or a good head on your shoulders is not likely to be enough these days. I would encourage you to consistently develop yourself. I assume by the fact that you picked up this book that you are in the right frame of mind to do that, but beyond this book, keep continuing to develop yourself.

It's never been easier to access information by the 'world's best' in any subject, and why wouldn't you want access to that information? I actively encourage, no, I insist that you learn regularly and invest in your skills and knowledge on sales, your sector, mindset, well-being, business, finance, marketing, or anything that's going to make you a more knowledgeable and well-rounded consultant and human being. Remember it's not just books that can help. There is also an abundance of information available in trade magazines or journals, on YouTube (try TED talks), Instagram or Twitter. If you are not much of a reader, then try audiobooks.

How and why?

If you are reading news related to your sector, then it can give you information that is relevant to the companies and people you speak with. This can make you come across as more of an expert. If you have up-to-date, relevant, topical knowledge of the things that matter to them, then you will establish rapport faster – after all, it is said that true rapport is made when someone believes you can help them.

"James, do you have any vacancies I can work on?" or "Tell me James, how do you think the increased government spending is likely to affect your business over the next year...."

Equally, if you are reading something about sales, about mindset, or anything from the self-help division, it's likely to have two effects: 1. You are likely to learn something new that you can try or apply and, 2. It will get your brain working!!!! I have found that some of my best work has come from when I am reading. I'll read something and think, "Ahh, that's cool. I wonder if that would work in our sector. How would I implement that?"

The point is, even if I read something that I think is just nonsense or not suitable for what I do, it almost always leads me on a path where I can come to the right conclusion about what is correct to do or try in the same situation.

Your commitment and how to implement it

If you are really serious about developing yourself to top-biller level, then this is yet another thing that's going to help make the difference. I ask you to commit to using at least one leg of your journey a day, either reading or studying, but remember to use what works for you. If you're not a reader or you ride a bike, for example, so you can't read, then listen to an audio program or speakers on YouTube. It could be motivational/mindset people like Tony Robbins or Jim Rohn, who I mentioned before, or leadership people like Simon

Sinek or John C Maxwell, or sales guys like Grant Cardone, Jordan Belfort or Chet Holmes.

Now, I have read several books about the need for personal development itself. Jim Rohn says, "There are three things to leave behind; your photographs, your library, and your personal journeys,", and I am sure you've heard the stat that the average CEO reads 60 books a year. What I get from this isn't necessarily knowledge (although I do) surprisingly; sometimes, I won't agree with the mindset of certain people or the way they go about things. For that matter, I am sure there will be lots in this book that you don't necessarily agree with or that won't work directly for your sector, and whist I have made every effort to make the content as broad and rich as I could, I am ok with that, just as along as what you do read is thought provoking, because that is where the growth is.

Make me one promise!

If you're not going to study on the way to work then make me one promise, don't go to sleep! If you are not going to learn, then that's your choice but do not sleep on the way to work. What kind of sedative state is that going to put you in before you arrive? So, with whatever you do, make sure you are actively getting your brain in the right mood.

So, if you are going to commit one leg of your journey, I would suggest you use the morning rather than the evening as you absorb more information in the morning. It will also help control your state so when you arrive at work you can hit it stronger. It's also worth noting that most of us are stronger mentally in the morning than we are in the afternoons so you should always start with your most challenging work and then, if you must, you can chill out or wind down with some music on the way home if you want to.

As usual though, whatever you commit to, commit to it and do it consistently!

> **My personal morning routine is as follows:**
>
> I walk to the station with my affirmations playing in my ears or speaking out loud.
>
> I arrive at the station and board a train.
>
> First thing when I'm on the train I text the wife to let her know I arrived and then I get straight to my goals. I write my goal list out in full each day in my goal book.
>
> I then have about 35 mins. of study time, which I mix up between reading a physical book and having the same audio book in my ears. When the book is finished, I jump on a week or so's worth of YouTube stuff.
>
> Then, just as the train arrives at the end station, I change to music (something upbeat, high energy or fast) so I can move my state up and get ready for the intensity of the morning.
>
> I walk through the door and no matter what mood I'm in or how I feel I or how tired I am, I bellow at the top of my voice, "GOOD MORNING. HOW ARE WE DOING TODAY, PEOPLE?".
>
> And then the day begins...

Chapter **25**

Consistency is key

If you ever visited my office, seen me speak, or dropped by as a fly on the wall, you will hear me say 'consistency is key' about 50 times a day. It is one of my standard go-to phrases that I am always ranting on about because I believe it is so true in our industry.

What I mean by this really is keep consistent.

As we have already discussed, there are many different things you're going to have to do within your role, and, as I said earlier in the book, my recommendation is to break them down into smaller tasks that are must-dos daily. If you must do them daily, then make sure you stay on top of them and don't finish the day until you have each of your tasks completed.

When I was building the business, for example, I used to have a check list simply called, "Can you go home yet?", and if you know me by now, I wouldn't go home until I could tick each thing.

Now, as I said before, your company is likely to have KPIs, stats or guides for almost every factor in your business. So, whatever you choose to do, whether you are placing one advert or fifty, whether you are making one call or one thousand, find your figure and keep consistent on that. If you can maintain a consistent level of input, then your level of output will be congruent with that, and that's when you can expect a level of result.

Find out what your KPIs are and tweak them, ideally by double. If that's not possible, then at least tweak them by twenty, thirty percent, and then make that *your* consistency. This will give you a few obvious advantages. 1. You will consistently overdeliver on your KPIs (which is something that will help you stay out of hot water if your sales are slow). 2. You will be able to work at a higher rate than your colleagues that work to minimums. 3. Your extra output will put you a level above your minimum-standard colleagues, and 4. Since your output is greater, you will learn faster as you will have covered more ground in the same time.

Once you have your standards and KPIs and whilst you're building your desk, keep to this level consistently. WARNING: Once you do this for a while you will start to see results and it is easy to busy yourself with other tasks thinking that you don't need these standards anymore. When you do this and you take your eye off the things that got you to that point, you end up with the yo-yo effect.

Chapter **26**

The yo-yo effect

The yo-yo effect is simply when you have one good month, one bad month, one good month, one bad month, up and down, over and over again just like a yo-yo on a string! Why does this happen? Well, you guessed it. You lost your consistency!

Because you are on a roll and you had or are having a good month, your focus comes away from generating new business and new candidates and goes into just delivering what you have. You get excited because you have got a good month, which is of course great, but at the same time you stop the consistency, you stop or reduce the adverts, the candidate work, the client calls, etc. Once your good month closes and the payday has gone, you quickly realise what you have done and you have nothing to work on, so you put the consistency back and then the pipeline grows, thus resulting in a future good month, and the process repeats.

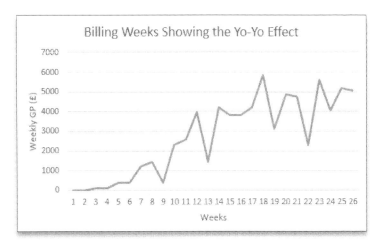

SJ RULE:-

Break the tasks down into smaller pieces. Work out what you are going to commit to and then be consistent on that. Every single day should be like clockwork. Order, structure, routine, discipline and consistency are key. If you can keep consistent, then you will build a solid sustainable desk.

Chapter **27**

Take action

Much like my last chapter about consistency, if you came by my office and I wasn't saying 'consistency is key', you would hear me yelling 'take action!'. It's another buzz phrase of mine. I absolutely love it and its application in every walk of life, especially in the business world. If you want to ponder and dwell on your own coin, well, that's your business to a degree. However, at work it is literally your contractual obligation to be as efficient as you can be.

Too many business hours and hundreds of thousands of pounds are spent pondering, wondering and delaying, so my rule is take action!

Once you have gathered enough information, and no more than enough, to do what you need to do, you must get going. There is no point delaying any further. If it's not going to work out, then the quickest, easiest and cheapest way to find out is to get moving, take action and get it started. You will find out if you are on the wrong path faster if you start walking, and then you can get moving on the right path.

Examples: If the client isn't going to pay and you have an awkward conversation to have, well, let's make the call and find out. We can all deal with it better once we know the lay of the land. If the candidate is not going to accept and it was a critical deal for you or the client, well, let's make the call and find out. Again, we will be better able to access our real options once we know!

Whatever is holding you back, there is zero benefit gained by waiting.

Don't delay what you can get done today and there is no better time than now.

"Time waits for no one."

"There is no better tomorrow than today."

There is an old saying is that there is no better tomorrow than today, and I believe that's applicable down to every minute of every day and in everything we do. If you are an overthinker, a time dweller or you are not sure what's going to happen, stop going on about it or thinking about the actions you could take and take *an* action.

Aside from increasing productivity and efficiency, you will find it's surprisingly refreshing and liberating.

That's exactly what I did with this book. I was talking about this for years and I've been telling people I was going to write a book until one day I stopped talking about it and I told myself I was going to take action.

I took a day off and I wrote the main flesh of the book in a day, the rest took around 9 months to complete, but the point was I got started. So, that's what you have to do. Decide what's important, when you are going to get it done, and then do it. It's simple as that. You should apply this to the big, long-term life decisions as well as the small daily ones that cloud our thinking.

Let me be the first to tell you to take an action. When you finish this book (you're nearly there), look back over it for a bit, highlight it, take some notes, agree on some things you can put in place, attempt or try, and then, you guessed it... take action on those things immediately. Now. Today or tomorrow, put them in place right away.

I feel you always get more out of a self-help book the second time around; however, if you are not reading it again, then shelf the book (or, better still, lend it to someone). If you are not reading it daily, write on your calendar for three or six months' time to revisit it and hold yourself accountable to the actions you said. You can list your actions in the last few pages.

Test yourself. Have you taken action on the things you said? Have you applied the things you were going to? See what else you can apply. If you got some value, then I want you to do two things. Pass the book on to the next person and see if it will help them, and then drop me a line to let me know what you achieved.

Chapter **28**

Effective advertising

One of the major differences about whether you're successful or not is likely to be how well you are able to attract talent. Naturally, the more talent you have coming through and the higher quality you have, the easier your life is going to be. One of the major ways we still do this is by placing adverts.

When you're placing your advert it's important to consider a few things. Hopefully, you know the job's spec or at least have a good understanding of the company that you're recruiting on behalf of and you know the role sufficiently to write something that represents it and the company well.

For most of us, we will be writing adverts that are not specific to the company, i.e. they won't be listing the company name. However, if you have a retainer (this is an upfront fee you charge for your work and work exclusively on behalf of a client) or you are working with a major client and you are able to do this, this will be an advantage to attract talent. However, it poses two major risks.

The candidate could always apply directly to the employer, thus losing your fee. Likewise, your rivals will be able to see your client and they will sell their candidates to your client or look to offer better terms than you. So, for the reasons listed above, in the most part we will be looking to place what I call a "specifically vague" advert – it needs to look genuine and promote the pros of the company and role without specifically naming anything that would render it obvious who the client is.

You need your applicant to feel like it's a genuine advert and so this is one of scenarios where you don't want to be using templates. It's okay to have a part of your advert placed as template, but you certainly don't want it to look like a template in the same way that you would read a script in a call centre but not want your caller to know you were reading a script. So, if your company offers templates to help with speed and efficiency then use that as an outline only.

The rest of the advert should be used to speak on behalf of the actual company, to speak about what the culture is like, the benefits are like, where it is, how easy is to get to, and all the usual things you would expect to see on an advert. Remember, be sure to reduce the specific elements.

A good reference point here is to look at the company's own website, see what they write about themselves, and the way they like to portray their company. Another good tip is to look at our rival agencies' websites for inspiration. How effective is their advertising? Is there stuff you can borrow? Is there stuff you definitely need to avoid? How do you compare against them? Finally, it's worth seeing if they have made either of the two major errors listed above. If they have, then there is some easy business development for you.

Finally, I would do the reverse job. Go to a search engine, act as if you are your ideal applicant, and type in the job they might be looking for. See what kind of adverts come up – this should help you tune if you are thinking in the right way.

Once you have your advert written and posted I would again go back to Google or the job board and search for it as an outsider. Does your advert come up? Does it look legible and genuine? If you were a suitable applicant would you click apply? This honest reflection is key.

SJ TIP

Have a good knowledge of the role and company

Place a specifically vague advert

Don't use a template or use only part of it

Check your rival agencies' websites for their adverts

Search for the job as if you were your ideal applicant and see what you get

Place your job advert and search for it as an applicant to see where you come

Repeat every three months or so

Chapter **29**

Use the path of least resistance

The Bruce Lee references are coming back from my childhood. I used to love a good Bruce Lee movie but it's an updated meaning that's applicable to our role.

What I mean is place the most placeable candidate even if that isn't the best candidate. In a fast-paced temp role, you're always going to find good, poor and average candidates. That will never change. However, if you have some control over which candidate is placed on top of your recommendations or which one goes foremost on your list, then place the one at the front who is the most placeable. N

Which one is the most placeable?

I mean the candidate that is in communication with you, that falls in the pay brackets that you'd like, that has rapport with you, that is on the same page, and that returns your calls, etc. If they all fall into this category (which is not very common), then place the cheapest in temps, and the most expensive in perms.

Too many consultants get hung up on the "perfect candidate" that they have no control over. Inevitably what happens is that you highlight how perfect your candidate is and, of course, the hiring manager says yes. They agree. They love

Use the path of least resistance

them and they request to bring them in for an interview. That's where the control breaks down (as we have discussed earlier).

Because you never had control over that candidate, making them not the most placeable, of course you get no call back from them and you get no commitment from them to turn up for the interview. Now you lose your image in front of the hiring manager. The opposite occurs in my situation. If you highlight the foremost one that has been your lead candidate, and you should always suggest the lead, then your interview request comes through for the most placeable candidate. The one that's most likely to get the deal is the one that's easiest to work with.

> **SJ Rule**
>
> Be like Bruce Lee, be like water and use the path of least resistance. Place the most placeable candidate, even if that candidate isn't the strongest.

Chapter **30**

End

So, there you have it. You've reached the end of the book. I sincerely and dearly hope that you learned something and I hope you got hundreds of thousands of pounds worth of value beyond the cost of this book. I genuinely hope that you've got something to take away from it. I hope that you've agreed to some actions for yourself and that you'll hold yourself accountable for committing those actions. I'd love to hear about the improvements that have been made in your billings or if you have managed to turn a corner and get on the right track.

I encourage you to make notes, to highlight, and to write in this book. I love to see a book that's been used as a manual to the industry. You can use it as a reference point later and I actively encourage you to pass it on to as many people as you can.

In my workplace, for example, we've implemented a work library where if you bring a self-help book in once you've finished it, you stick it in on the shelf and allow others to share the knowledge. If you have something similar, I'd love to become part of your library and to have your recommendation.

Polite Review Request

This has been an ambition achieved to actually write, complete, and publish a book.

If you got some value out of it, you made a further step in your career, or you've secured your recruitment job when you couldn't do so before,

If you passed your probation when you were on the verge, or if you have really started to get more DMs on the phone and you broke a record or made top biller status, I would be absolutely over the moon and grateful for any review you leave.

It obviously helps me power the book and get more publicity around it so that it can reach more people quicker, but beyond that it would make my day to know that it helped you.

If you do feel compelled enough to give a review then I asked you to 'take action' and do it now or if you have any feedback, feel free to contact me directly through my LinkedIn page where I will personally respond to you.

https://www.linkedin.com/in/stephen-joseph-a5637442/?originalSubdomain=uk

Finally, this just leaves me to wrap up the book and say congratulations for finishing the book, congratulations on Securing, Surviving and Thriving in your 12 months in recruitment, and I hope one day our paths will cross, until then, I wish you the very best of luck in your career.

Thank you

Firstly, to Vic Johnson, author of "How to Write a Book this Weekend", who gave me the tools and information to get this idea out of my head and into action. If I didn't have that book, you wouldn't have this book, so if you have a book in your head, then I thoroughly recommend you read that book, and whist it didn't take a weekend(more like 9 months for me), it did get done, and it's easier than you think.

I also have to thank Stefan Ivanovic who helped convert the initial transcription. He is available via upwork.com and if you need any transcription work. I recommend him completely.

I would also like to thank Aimy K and Laeeq Hussain Immaculate Studios who designed the cover for me.

I also owe a large thank you to Lee Ellis my editor who converted my scribble into something that humans could read! Lee really did a fantastic job helping with the flow, spelling, grammar, jargon, punctuation, terminology, semantics and formatting. Without him and his expertise the book would still be on my laptop! Thank you, Lee, and again if you need any editing work you can contact him via upwork.com also.

NOTES PAGE

....

....

....

....

....

....

....

....

....

....

....

....

....

....

....

Printed in Great Britain
by Amazon